BUILDING A SL
A RAND Project tc

M000290549

China
AND THE
International Order

Michael J. Mazarr
Timothy R. Heath
Astrid Stuth Cevallos

Prepared for the Office of Net Assessment, Office of the Secretary of Defense

For more information on this publication, visit www.rand.org/t/RR2423

Library of Congress Cataloging-in-Publication Data is available for this publication.
ISBN: 978-1-9774-0062-8

Published by the RAND Corporation, Santa Monica, Calif.
© Copyright 2018 RAND Corporation
RAND® is a registered trademark.

Cover image by Kagenmi/stock.adobe.com

Support RAND
Make a tax-deductible charitable contribution at
www.rand.org/giving/contribute

www.rand.org

Preface

This report is part of a larger RAND study on the future of the post–World War II liberal international order. The overall project is examining the theoretical and historical foundations of the order, its current status and prospects, and policy options for the future. This report represents our analysis of China's approach to a multilateral order and draws implications from that analysis for future U.S. policy.

This research was sponsored by the Office of Net Assessment in the Office of the Secretary of Defense and conducted within the International Security and Defense Policy Center of the RAND National Defense Research Institute, a federally funded research and development center sponsored by the Office of the Secretary of Defense, the Joint Staff, the Unified Combatant Commands, the Navy, the Marine Corps, the defense agencies, and the defense Intelligence Community.

For more information on the RAND International Security and Defense Policy Center, see www.rand.org/nsrd/ndri/centers/isdp or contact the Center director (contact information is provided on the webpage).

Contents

Tables

Summary

This report evaluates the character and possible future of China's engagement with the post–World War II international order. The resulting portrait is anything but straightforward: China's engagement with the order remains a complex and often contradictory work in progress. In the Maoist era, China frequently maintained an antagonistic posture to the international system. However, since the advent of the reform and opening-up period in the late 1970s, the trajectory of China's policy toward the postwar order has been more supportive. It has joined hundreds of leading institutions, gradually boosted its direct and indirect support for many multilateral activities and norms, and expressed a commitment to increasing its role in global governance.

However, following precedents set by other great powers, China as an increasingly powerful nation has also demonstrated a willingness to challenge and revise aspects of the existing order. In some cases, it has created institutions, such as the Asian Infrastructure Investment Bank (AIIB), that are more responsive to Chinese interests but may duplicate existing institutions—suggesting competition. On other issues, such as human rights, Beijing has conditioned its support on a redefinition of key terms to reflect China's preferences. In still other cases, such as trade and nonproliferation, China has supported key norms—but its behavior falls far short of complete compliance and, in some cases (as in its industrial policy), seems actively calculated to circumvent the spirit of the norms.

This report evaluates the character and possible future of China's engagement with the postwar international order as part of a larger RAND study on the future of the postwar liberal international order, the Project on Building a Sustainable International Order. To make this assessment, the analysis examined China's participation in international institutions, adherence to international norms, compliance with established rule sets, and broad level of support for multilateral coordination and problem-solving under the aegis of the postwar order. RAND researchers consulted available evidence on China's behavior in these areas; analyzed Chinese official documents and scholarly writings; reviewed recent activities and trends; gathered data on several especially important issue areas, such as evidence of Chinese compliance with nonproliferation and activities within the United Nations (UN); and brought together a number of subject-matter experts for a roundtable to evaluate key evidence.

The biggest wild card is the question of where China's policy is headed over the medium term, roughly the next decade. The directives contained in the 19th Party Congress suggest that China intends to adopt a bolder approach toward questions of international leadership, becoming more deeply involved in key institutions and issues, such as peacekeeping and climate change. At the same time, China may also step up efforts to challenge norms favoring liberal democratic values that it has long opposed. Because China is unlikely to surpass the United States by virtually any measure of national power any time soon, China is unlikely to displace the United States as the global norm-setting power. However, China's burgeoning power is already intensifying competition with the United States for leadership and influence within the international system, primarily at the regional level but also increasingly at the global level. Indeed, on select issue areas (such as climate change) and in some geographic areas (such as some countries affected by the overland Silk Road Economic Belt and 21st Century Maritime Silk Road [known as the Belt and Road Initiative]), Chinese influence could surpass that of the United States. Whether a growing competition for influence and leadership with the United States in shaping the terms of the international order escalates into dynamics that become destructive of that order remains to be determined.

One major challenge in this study, therefore, is that the question of China's future approach to the international order is bound up inextricably with broader strategic questions regarding the evolution of Chinese power, the vitality of the international system, and the firmness of the U.S. commitment to leading that international order. The evolution of these variables cannot be predicted with confidence. Any analysis of China's approach to a shared international order—and possibly U.S. strategy and policy responses to that approach—must take seriously the fact that it is dealing with a moving target. Currently available data and interpretations do not allow an unqualified medium-term judgment.

Taking this larger context into account—as well as the complexity of China's behavior to date—this study offers three major findings about the relationship of China to the international order.

First, *China can be expected to demand more influence in the international system as a condition for its support.* Broadly speaking, since China undertook a new policy of international engagement in the 1980s—and putting aside the areas (liberal values and human rights) in which the Chinese Communist Party has the greatest degree of conflict with the U.S.-led order—the level and quality of its participation in the order rival those of most other nations. It has come to see multilateral institutions and processes as important, if not essential, for the achievement of its interests. However, like the United States and other major powers, an increasingly powerful China has demanded exceptions to the rules and norms when it sees vital interests at stake. Moreover, as its role in the international community grows, China will likely demand changes to institutions and norms to reflect its power and value preferences as a condition for its support. Indeed, at the 19th Party Congress in 2017, President Xi Jinping called for China to become a "global leader" in terms of comprehensive national power and "international influence" by mid-century. However, these demands are not likely to contest the fundamental nature of the international system.

Second, looking forward, *a strengthened and increasingly multilateral international order can continue to provide a critical tool for the United States and other countries to shape and constrain rising Chinese power.* The growing collective strength of the developing world opens opportunities for the United States to engage these countries as partners in building a more-resilient international order. This is true for two major reasons. First, reforms that accommodate the interests of rising powers through greater multilateralism can make the international system more responsive and robust. Second, a widely supported multilateral system provides the United States with greater leverage: Involvement by more countries can also help fashion norms against which individual countries are judged for their status, prestige, and influence. This can, in turn, incentivize China to participate and restrain its behavior or risk prompting a multilateral balancing process grounded in the norms of a mutually agreed order. Examples of reforms to build multilateralism and strengthen norms include measures to expand the role of China and other developing economies in the International Monetary Fund (IMF) and to increase Chinese involvement in mediating international conflicts through the UN. Reforms to accommodate the interests of China and other rising powers alone are unlikely to determine Chinese behavior. Strong U.S. leadership, backed by military strength and in cooperation with its network of allies and partners, will remain essential to deterring China from considering the most egregious and dangerous acts of aggression against its neighbors. However, a resilient and responsive multilateral order can play a critical role in incentivizing China to operate primarily within, as opposed to outside, international institutions.

Finally, *modifications to the order on the margins in response to Chinese preferences will typically pose less of a threat to a stable international system than a future in which China is alienated from that system.* Some observers have expressed concern about the implications of alternative standards or institutions promoted by China, such as the establishment of the AIIB, to enable development-related investments in Asia without the conditions (in terms of human rights, rule of law, or labor or environmental standards) that typically accompany efforts by the existing Asian Development Bank. Although Chinese-led initiatives do challenge U.S. leadership and influence, they generally do not pose a threat to the fundamental integrity of the international system. Because an international system that features a greater Chinese presence but remains stable and effective would favor U.S. interests more than a conflict-ridden international system in which China is alienated, the United States should seek ways to participate in Chinese-led initiatives and appropriately expand opportunities for Chinese involvement in existing institutions.

In considering China's future role in the order, the United States can take reassurance from the high degree of legitimacy and trust in the international system expressed by most countries, although polls do indicate that China has made remarkable strides in narrowing the gap in favorability with the United States in the past few years.[1] By many measures, including gross domestic product and defense spending, the United States will remain the world's most powerful country for the foreseeable future and thus will remain the most essential leader in the international order. Overall, China has viewed U.S. leadership as having contributed to international peace and prosperity in some important ways, even if its differences with the United States have grown over time.

China's role in shaping Asia's economic and security order is likely to be the most contentious part of its foreign policy in the future. China's determination to become Asia's paramount power will unavoidably entail an intensifying competition for influence with the United States. Balancing Chinese power and protecting U.S. interests will remain challenging tasks, especially given the fact that the realities of economic integration have rendered Cold War–style strategies of containment infeasible. However, the outcome is hardly foreordained. China's ability to realize its ambition is constrained by the fact that many Asian countries remain distrustful of Chinese power. To the extent that Beijing attempts to assert regional dominance through efforts that fail to adequately account for the interests of other countries, it will produce—and is already producing—countervailing reactions from regional states. Therefore, there are limits to how much China can use major geopolitical economic initiatives, such as the infrastructure and trade effort, to link Europe, Africa, and China through the Belt and Road Initiative to bribe or coerce participating nations into doing its bidding. In addition to formidable challenges to sustaining economic

---

[1]   Margaret Vice, "In Global Popularity Contest, U.S. and China—Not Russia—Vie for First Place," Pew Research Center, August 23, 2017.

growth, China thus faces many hurdles in its efforts to shape an economic and security order in Asia to its advantage.

In sum, this study argues for a two-part U.S. approach to the future of China's engagement with the international order.

First, the United States should develop a comprehensive strategy to sustain and expand China's role in the international order. This strategy should include efforts both to accommodate China in existing global institutions, such as the IMF, and for the United States and others to participate in Chinese-led initiatives, such as the AIIB and Belt and Road Initiative. This recommendation flows from a more-general assumption: The growth of Chinese power is not something the United States can or should oppose per se but instead should seek to steer in a direction that reinforces existing institutions and norms. In the process, the United States should use expanded cooperation to build strong, long-term relationships with Chinese officials at all levels and in all issue areas, even as it continues to affirm relations with its allies and partners.

To be clear, this recommendation does not assume that such efforts will ease Chinese demands or reduce the degree of assertiveness with which it pushes territorial or other claims. This analysis presumes the opposite—that growing Chinese power and self-confidence will produce an era of rising Sino-American tension and rivalry. In such a context, the primary U.S. strategic challenge is neither to "prevent" China's rise nor to appease its demands so fundamentally as to prevent such a rivalry. The challenge is to manage the emerging rivalry in ways that avoid major conflict, leave open the potential for cooperation on as many issues of mutual concern as possible, and safeguard vital U.S. interests. Encouraging China to uphold the rules, norms, and institutions of a shared order—while working simultaneously to sustain the coalition of mostly like-minded democracies at the core of that order to bolster U.S. influence—can be a central element of a strategy to achieve those goals.

Second, the United States should continue to dissuade China from employing various forms of violent aggression to fulfill its regional ambitions. While many of China's specific claims and actions are designed to skirt rather than directly violate formal international law, the country's efforts could increasingly threaten norms of territorial nonaggression and risk regional conflict to the extent that China becomes much more belligerent in the pursuit of them. Regional states are not naive about the possible forms of Chinese muscle-flexing and continue to look to the United States to play an essential role in deterrence. Therefore, the second component of U.S. strategy centers on ensuring military readiness to exercise credible deterrence against aggressive challenges to the international order. Also, in select cases involving core values regarding human rights and democracy, the United States should reaffirm its commitment to norms that reflect those values and resist Chinese efforts to change them—but in a measured way that builds on common values and concerns.

Acknowledgments

The authors would like to thank the sponsor for its support of the project and intellectual guidance throughout, including detailed comments on the final draft report. We would also like to thank a number of anonymous China specialists, from both within and outside RAND, who gathered in May 2016 for discussion of an earlier version of this analysis; their comments have been tremendously helpful in finalizing our findings. We appreciate the reviewers for this report, including Thomas Christensen of Princeton University and Michael Chase and Chris Chivvis of RAND. Finally, we offer our grateful appreciation to Seth Jones, the former project manager in the International Security and Defense Program, for his project management supervision of this effort from the beginning. We could not have hoped for a more helpful and congenial program manager.

Abbreviations

ABMT	Anti–Ballistic Missile Treaty
AIIB	Asian Infrastructure Investment Bank
APEC	Asian-Pacific Economic Cooperation
ASEAN	Association of Southeast Asian Nations
BRICS	Brazil, Russia, India, China, and South Africa
CCP	Chinese Communist Party
CICA	Conference on Interaction and Confidence Building
CICIR	Chinese Institute for Contemporary International Relations
CTBT	Comprehensive Test Ban Treaty
EEZ	exclusive economic zone
FDI	foreign direct investment
G-20	Group of Twenty
ILO	International Labor Organization
IMF	International Monetary Fund
IP	intellectual property
MID	militarized interstate dispute
NGO	nongovernmental organization
NPT	Nuclear Nonproliferation Treaty
NSC	National Security Council

ODA	overseas development aid
OECD	Organisation of Economic Co-operation and Development
PCA	Permanent Court of Arbitration
PLA	People's Liberation Army
PRC	People's Republic of China
RCEP	Regional Comprehensive Economic Partnership
SCO	Shanghai Cooperation Organization
SDR	Special Drawing Right
THAAD	Terminal High Altitude Aerial Defense
UN	United Nations
UNCLOS	United Nations Convention of the Law of the Sea
WB	World Bank
WTO	World Trade Organization

CHAPTER ONE

Introduction

At a Politburo study session on global governance on October 12, 2015, Chinese President Xi Jinping declared that the "fundamental purpose" for China's "participation in global governance" is to "serve the achievement of the Chinese Dream of the great rejuvenation of the Chinese nation."[1] The ambiguity of that statement and the conflicting signals available in China's recent behavior capture the uncertainty with which many observers regard an increasingly powerful China's approach to the post–World War II international order. What does China require of the world to achieve its announced goal of revitalization? What will China's revitalization mean for the international order?

This study is one component of a larger RAND effort, the Project on Building a Sustainable International Order,[2] to examine the character, status, and possible future of that postwar order. Previous reports in this study have attempted to define that order, assess its current health, and examine alternative directions it could take and their implications. This report represents an analysis of China's interests, behavior, and future prospects to evaluate both the recent history of its interaction with the international order and possible future trajectories. It seeks to discern how China has approached the international order in past decades and how its approach might change as the country grows to become one of the world's most powerful. The study also hopes to

---

[1] "At the 27th Collective Study Session of the CCP Political Bureau; Xi Jinping Stresses the Need to Push Forward the System of Global Governance," *Xinhua*, October 13, 2015.

[2] The project description and publications can be found at www.rand.org/nsrd/projects/international-order.

illuminate opportunities for the United States and identify areas that could be of concern.

The question of how China's rise will affect the international order carries considerable significance for the future of global politics. A well-established literature illustrates the perils of transitions between rising and established great powers, but it remains unclear whether China and the United States will also clash.[3] Some observers have suggested that China seeks to "overturn" the international order. For example, Michael Pillsbury claimed that China has a "secret plan" to overthrow U.S. hegemony and establish its dominion over the world.[4] Martin Jacques outlined a vision of a Chinese-led global order.[5] Other experts have questioned whether China has the will or ability to overturn the established order. Michael Swaine concluded that China seeks to reform, but uphold, the current order.[6] David Shambaugh doubted that China has the capability to contest global leadership, noting the country's limited power and influence and its "passive and narrow-minded" approach to diplomacy.[7] Thomas Christensen paints a complex and nuanced portrait of China's interaction with the international order, but he worries that "Beijing's unfortunate combination of external confidence and internal anxiety" could spark more belligerent policies.[8]

A China that broadly supports key norms of the order and works toward stability and prosperity—even if it frequently disagrees with the United States and seeks to expand its own influence—could help to preserve essential elements of a stable international order. A China that

---

[3] Henk Houlewig, "Power Transition as a Cause of War," *Journal of Conflict Resolution*, Vol. 32, March 1988.

[4] Michael Pillsbury, *The Hundred Year Marathon: China's Secret Strategy to Replace America as the Global Superpower*, New York: Henry Holt and Co., 2015.

[5] Martin Jacques, *When China Rules the World*, New York: Penguin Books, 2012.

[6] Michael Swaine, "Chinese Views on Global Governance Since 2008–2009: Not Much New," *China Leadership Monitor*, February 8, 2016.

[7] David Shambaugh, "The Illusion of Chinese Power," Brookings Institution, June 25, 2014.

[8] Thomas J. Christensen, *The China Challenge: Shaping the Choices of a Rising Power*, New York: W. W. Norton, 2016, p. 244.

is determined to undermine many of the order's institutions, replace them with Sinocentric alternatives, and press sovereignty claims even at the risk of war could cause the order to either collapse or devolve into violent confrontation, especially between China and the United States. China's stance on the order will be decisive in determining the order's future.

The evidence on what China might do in the future remains mixed. In official statements, China's leaders have said that they support international institutions but oppose the Western liberal democratic values and the system of military alliances that underpin the "U.S.–led world order."[9] Like any powerful country, China's leaders are likely to use the country's growing influence to shape the rules of the order to serve their interests and to circumvent those rules that do not.[10] Which institutions and rules of the order will China's leaders continue to support, and which ones will they seek to change? Which of the potential changes could threaten the interests of the United States?

To gain insight on these questions, this report surveys the existing academic literature on China's rise, its participation in international institutions, and its regional security activities. It also weighs the People's Republic of China's (PRC's) behavior, PRC official statements, and articles published in government-sponsored news media to support judgments about China's potential future attitudes and actions toward the order. Although this report does not provide a comprehensive account of official and unofficial Chinese views of international

---

[9]   Fu Ying, "China No Threat to International Order," China-U.S. Focus, February 15, 2016b. For other sources on China's broad approach to the international order, see Yong Deng, "The Post-Responsible Power," *Washington Quarterly*, Vol. 37, No. 4, Winter 2015; Gregory Chin and Ramesh Thakur, "Will China Change the Rules of Global Order?" *Washington Quarterly*, Vol. 33, No. 4, October 2010, pp. 165–195; and Thomas J. Christensen, "Fostering Stability or Creating a Monster? The Rise of China and U.S. Policy Toward East Asia," *International Security*, Vol. 31, No. 1, 2006.

[10]   Michael Swaine, "Beyond American Predominance in the Western Pacific: The Need for a Stable U.S.-China Balance of Power," Carnegie Endowment for International Peace, April 20, 2015; Swaine, 2016; Andrew J. Nathan, "China's Rise and International Regimes: Does China Seek to Overthrow Global Norms?" in Robert S. Ross and Jo Inge Bekkevold, eds., *China in the Era of Xi Jinping: Domestic and Foreign Policy Challenges*, Washington, D.C.: Georgetown University Press, 2016.

order, it summarizes them, drawing from publications that explore these views in detail.

The complexity of the international order and the variety of its components pose an unavoidable challenge to any analysis of China's approach. Like many leading states, China participates in a large number of the order's institutions and processes and observes many of its norms and rules. However, China also opposes a handful of prominent norms and institutions, such as the value of human rights, liberal democracy, and security based on military alliances. Like other great powers, China's rule compliance has been uneven on issues that bear on its national interests.

A major reason for the difficulty of carrying out such an assessment lies in the complexity of the international order—or multiple types of order—to which China is reacting. China's general support for the global economic order, for example, contrasts with its skepticism regarding aspects of the global political order, such as human rights conventions. Its approach to parts of the global security order has evolved over time. In some cases, as in coping with the threat of international piracy, China has moved toward greater cooperation. In others, such as the role of the U.S. alliance system in Asia, China's stance has grown more critical. Therefore, it is not entirely accurate to speak of China's interaction with "the" international order—its posture has been highly differentiated depending on the component of the order.

The Chinese case also suggests that a country changes its strategic intentions, at least in part, in response to changes in the structure of international politics. As economic power diffuses across more countries and China becomes more dependent on the world economy, China is being forced to abandon its long-standing, largely passive approach to global governance. This report aims to illuminate how China's leaders are responding to this conundrum by pursuing a more active form of international leadership in the near, mid, and long terms.

Finally, our analysis suggests that one distinction has increasingly come to dominate China's attitude toward the international order: the difference between the United Nations-centric (UN-centric) order based on sovereignty and the U.S.-dominated liberal order focused on human rights and U.S. alliance structures. China's support for the former has been consistent and seems likely to remain so as long as its growing power can be accommodated by the system—something that will require some degree of special treatment for China, as it has for the United States since 1945. However, China has also become increasingly strident in its denunciations of an order in which Washington plays a disproportionate role in making and enforcing the rules. China's attitude toward international order depends heavily on which of these orders is at issue. The critical implication is that challenges to U.S. hegemony need not imply challenges to some form of rule-based order that constrains China's power. Distinguishing the two will be a critical challenge for U.S. diplomacy in the years ahead.

Within the context of these constraints and considerations, China's potential interaction with the international order is likely to unfold in stages. In the near term (zero to five years), China is advocating reforms to improve the responsiveness and effectiveness of existing international organizations and processes. Efforts to promote a favorable set of values, norms, and principles as an ideological foundation for a reformed order may bear fruit in the medium term (five to ten years). While working through existing organizations and institutions where feasible, China is also establishing alternatives better suited to its needs. Long-term (more than ten years) effects are less well defined, in part because the Chinese continue to debate the way ahead. However, while many of these measures may take years to carry out at the global level, Beijing has already started efforts to restructure the Asia-Pacific regional order because of its proximity to China and its importance for Chinese strategic interests. Therefore, Chinese policies at the regional level could provide insight into the likely trajectory of the country's foreign policies at the global level.

Defining the International Order

To grasp China's attitude toward the postwar international order, we must first define what we mean by that term. An *order*, we argued in an earlier report for this project, "is a stable, structured pattern of rela-

tionships among states that involves some combination of parts, ranging from emergent norms to rule-making institutions to international
political organizations or regimes."[11] An order is differentiated from the
more-general concept of an international system by this settled, structured character. G. John Ikenberry similarly defines an *order* as a set
of "governing arrangements between states, including its fundamental
rules, principles, and institutions."[12]

We began this project most concerned with the effects of state
behavior on the specific normative and institutional elements of the
current pattern of relationships—what might be called the "institutional order." The institutional order comprises such elements as key
international organizations—including the UN, the International
Monetary Fund (IMF), World Bank (WB), and the World Trade
Organization (WTO)—that provide forums for collective dialogue
and action and for managing such key issues as financial stability; the
large set of multilateral treaties, agreements, and conventions establishing rules on issues ranging from trade to human rights; and networks
of informal organizations and networks. In a longer-term sense, it also
incorporates the socialization effects and norms of behavior that arise
in connection with the institutional order.

Yet, as we have worked through the study, we have become increasingly more aware that the full character of the postwar order reflects
two aspects beyond a list of its major institutions. First, it embodies
the broader principle of multilateralism that has long characterized the
U.S. vision of world politics. As John Ruggie has defined it, a *multilateral order* "embodies rules of conduct that are commonly applicable
to all countries," rather than discriminatory ones. It recognizes shared
interests among states and offers mechanisms for "joint action."[13] The

---

[11]   Michael J. Mazarr, Miranda Priebe, Andrew Radin, and Astrid Stuth Cevallos, *Understanding the Current International Order*, Santa Monica, Calif.: RAND Corporation, RR-
1598-OSD, 2016.

[12]   G. John Ikenberry, *After Victory: Institutions, Strategic Restraint, and the Rebuilding of
Order After Major Wars*, Princeton, N.J.: Princeton University Press, 2001, p. 23.

[13]   John G. Ruggie, "Third Try at World Order? America and Multilateralism After the Cold
War," *Political Science Quarterly*, Vol. 109, No. 4, 1994. pp. 556–557.

value of the order lies in part in the potential significance of this larger vision and the degree to which actual events have achieved part of its promise.

Another influential element of the postwar order lies in the core group of like-minded states, a group that endorses some degree of shared order and that together reflects a critical mass of power and purpose in the international sphere. The institutional order has become the connective tissue for a group of largely like-minded states, built around the core set of value-sharing democracies.[14] This group has gradually come to reflect an embryonic and incomplete form of international community, with a very real appreciation for their shared fate, the benefits of cooperation where possible, and the costs of aggressive or selfish action. The result has been the emergence of a critical mass of countries that create a gravitational pull with disproportionate global influence. When combined with conditions for joining the core group, this situation can affect preferences and behavior.[15]

When we conceive of the postwar order, therefore, this project has at least three major components in mind: its specific institutions, rules, and norms (the "institutional order"); the ways in which the principle and practice of multilateralism shape world politics; and the attractive and sometimes coercive influence of the predominant collection of value-sharing states that represent the core membership of the order. The true effects of any international order can only be understood by considering this fusion of components—the institutional order, the principles of state conduct it reflects, and the combined preferences of the community of states that comprise its membership. These three elements taken together make up what should be understood as the prevailing global order.

Finally, our research has also illustrated how the overarching postwar international order can be usefully conceived as a number of specific suborders, each with its own characteristics and degree of

---

[14] Michael J. Mazarr, "Preserving the Postwar Order," *Washington Quarterly*, Vol. 40, No. 2, Summer 2017.

[15] Quddus V. Snyder, "Integrating Rising Powers: Liberal Systemic Theory and the Mechanism of Cooperation," *Review of International Studies*, Vol. 39, 2013.

influence. These include at least three different economic suborders: the trade order, the financial and monetary order, and the development order. There are at least three security suborders: the UN Charter–based nonaggression order, the multilateral security order built on shared interests in areas like nonproliferation and counterpiracy, and the U.S.-led system of alliances. There is also a global liberal values order that consists primarily of human rights conventions, as well as informal norms that underpin many institutions.

One of the most important findings of this report is that China approaches many of these components differently.[16] It has different interests within and different perspectives with respect to several suborders, including the global political order based on the guarantees of sovereignty and nonaggression reflected in the UN Charter, as well as the associated UN system of departments, committees, and treaties; the global trade order; the financial and monetary order; the multilateral security order, including nonproliferation treaties and cooperation on counterterrorism; and the U.S.-led security order, composed largely of the regional and global alliance systems. The evidence surveyed in the following chapters suggests a significant distinction between China's approach to the first four of these suborders and the final one. Like all major powers, China's approach to any one suborder has been complicated and reflects some degree of contradiction. Broadly speaking, however, the trajectory of its engagement with the first four suborders has been largely positive, whereas its attitude toward the U.S. security order (and hallmarks of U.S. predominance in the other orders) has become increasingly competitive. Managing this tension is among the most important challenges in shaping China's future engagement with international order.

---

[16] Alastair Iain Johnston, "China and International Order: Which China? Which Order?" paper presented at the conference "Negotiating the Future: Visions of Global Order," German Institute of Global and Area Studies, Hamburg, Germany, December 3–4, 2015.

Methodology and Approach

In order to evaluate the history, present status, and potential future trajectories of China's attitude and behavior toward the postwar international order, we conducted qualitative analysis of several forms of data: historical analysis, statements of Chinese officials and official documents, empirical evidence of China's behavior, and existing subject-matter expert studies of China's attitude toward the postwar order. As in most analyses for the overall RAND project on the international order, we reviewed extensive data on national behavior; ultimately, we found that questions about China's strategy could not be answered through quantitative analysis.[17] Data can provide evidence on specific points, but no statistical analysis of data sets will provide an unambiguous picture of China's past, present, or future posture. Therefore, our conclusions represent informed qualitative inferential interpretation of existing data.

First, we reviewed the primary national interests that China is pursuing through its engagement with any international order. These interests shape China's assessment of the potential utility of the components of order. An important theme for the study as a whole is that a state can discover many ways of pursuing the ends reflected in its national interests, and a well-functioning international order can help shape a state's decisions about the most effective ways of doing so. For example, a working international trade and financial order may provide avenues to national prosperity that might be preferable to alternatives and that might not exist without those components of order. On the other hand, some states conceive of their interests in ways that reject the demands of a multilateral order in whole or part, thus preventing them from taking advantage of the potential advantages of such an order. Therefore, a definition of national interests does not provide unambiguous evidence for how a state will approach an international order, but it is a crucial starting point.

Second, we reviewed evidence about China's explicit attitude toward the postwar order and how it may be changing. This evidence

---

[17]   Mazarr et al., 2016.

includes official Chinese documents, the statements of senior officials in the Chinese government, and ideas expressed in unofficial but
government-affiliated publications. We reviewed both English- and
Chinese-language sources for such evidence.

Third, we evaluated China's actual behavior toward elements of
the international order since 1945. These included China's participation in leading institutions and its behavior in relation to key norms of
the order. We evaluated this behavior according to objective criteria as
applied to each of the five suborders mentioned earlier. The resulting
analyses remain qualitative, although they are grounded in data about
Chinese behavior.

Fourth, we reviewed discussions of the future trajectory of China's international role and policies, as well as the four alternatives for
international order described in an earlier report of this project.[18] From
these resources, we derived a spectrum of possible Chinese approaches
to order and evaluated their likelihood, narrowing to four feasible
alternative future scenarios. We evaluated the implications of each for
U.S. policy and identified the steps most useful for hedging against the
range of possibilities.

Fifth, we reviewed interim findings on these issues at a roundtable
with subject-matter experts held at the RAND offices in Arlington,
Virginia. We received comments on an earlier version of this work and
clarified key factual questions about China's actions.

We present the findings of this research in four sections. Chapter Two provides an analysis of China's national interests and strategic intentions as a way of understanding the objectives it is likely to
have when interacting with the international order. Drawing on official
and unofficial reports and publications, Chapter Three surveys China's
views of the prevailing order. Chapter Four examines China's behavior
with respect to different components of the order. It assesses whether
China has been supportive, hostile, or indifferent to specific international institutions, norms, and practices. Chapter Five examines how

---

[18] Michael J. Mazarr, Miranda Priebe, Andrew Radin, and Astrid Stuth Cevallos, *Alternative Options for U.S. Policy Toward the International Order*, Santa Monica, Calif.: RAND
Corporation, RR-2011-OSD, 2017.

this behavior might be changing. It examines trends in current and prospective Chinese approaches to the order, and it draws from an earlier report in this project series to posit four possible trajectories for China's approach to the international order and the policy implications of each for the United States. Chapter Six offers general conclusions and recommendations.

CHAPTER TWO

China's Interests and Ambitions

The fundamental context for China's current and prospective stance on the international order is set by its national interests—and, more specifically, its subjective perception of those interests at any given time and its leaders' beliefs about the most-effective ways of achieving them. For any country, the value of the international order lies in the way it can facilitate the pursuit of national interests. China's engagement with the order thus far suggests that the country has pursued key interests, including prosperity, security, and prestige, by taking advantage of the economic and political opportunities offered by the current international order.

This chapter reviews China's current conception of its essential national, or core, interests. The following chapter assesses how these interests, as well as other factors, shape China's view of the postwar international order.

China's Core Interests

Since the early 2000s, China's leaders have focused on three important national, or what authorities call "core," interests (核心利益): security, sovereignty, and development. According to the 2011 Peaceful Development White Paper, the first interest (security) refers to the country's fundamental protection from danger and chaos. Threats to security include both existential threats, such as those posed by nuclear annihilation, and potential challenges to the nation's integrity and stability, such as those posed by terrorists or separatists. Security also includes the maintenance of the country's political system, defined by Chinese Communist Party (CCP) rule. Sovereignty includes the interests of national sovereignty, which refers to the country's ability to exercise authority over all geographic claims, including Taiwan. It also includes territory, which refers to the integrity of all land and maritime borders. Threats to sovereignty include challenges by rival claimants to disputed territory. The core interest of development refers to access to the resources and goods required for the country to sustain economic development. Threats to development include disruption of key shipping lanes and instability in distant countries that could interrupt China's access to important natural resources and markets.[1] Chinese documents and leaders' statements vary in their descriptions of the core interests, but the concepts provide the essential framework through which China evaluates the utility and effectiveness of the international order. Table 2.1 summarizes the core interests.

China's leaders' top priority is to maintain CCP control. Any attempt to undermine the party's legitimacy is perceived as threatening. Since the 1970s, the CCP has moved away from its earlier emphasis on socialist ideology and toward economic growth and competent governance as its source of legitimacy. This successful shift toward performance-based legitimacy has strengthened the party's grip on power, despite its nominal adherence to an antiquated Marxist ideology and Leninist politics.[2]

Chinese leaders recognize that ensuring economic growth and defending China's sovereignty and territory are critical to maintaining public support. Thus, China has shown a growing willingness to help curb transnational threats to international trade, such as maritime piracy. It has also challenged international norms that undermine China's efforts to control its interests in the near seas, such as the 2016

---

[1]   Information Office of the State Council, "China's Peaceful Development," white paper, People's Republic of China, September 21, 2011.

[2]   See discussion in Andrew J. Nathan, "Authoritarian Resilience," *Journal of Democracy*, Vol. 14, No. 1, January 2003, pp. 13–14. He cites multiple additional factors that influence CCP legitimacy, including the development of local-level institutions—such as village elections—that have given Chinese citizens the feeling that their concerns are being taken into consideration in the policymaking process.

Table 2.1
China's Core Interests

Interest	Components	Relevant Threats
Security	• Basic national security • Maintenance of the basic political system	• Existential dangers, such as nuclear attack, as well as challenges to social stability from terrorists and separatists • Challenges to CCP rule and values
Sovereignty	• Sovereignty over all claimed geography • Territorial integrity, including maritime and land boundaries	• Threats to the government's exercise of authority include Taiwan • Rival claimants to disputed land
Development	• Access to natural resources and markets • Key shipping lanes. Threats include international piracy	• Instability near vital energy sources • International piracy

SOURCE: Information Office of the State Council, 2011.

ruling by the International Tribunal for Law of the Sea regarding the South China Sea.[3] Chinese leaders also oppose norms that legitimize foreign intervention, such as the "responsibility to protect," democracy and human rights promotion, and freedom of information, fearing that foreign countries will use these tools to undermine the CCP's authority or Chinese efforts to unify with Taiwan. President Xi summarized China's stance on sovereignty during his September 2015 speech to the UN General Assembly:

> The principle of sovereignty not only means that the sovereignty and territorial integrity of all countries are inviolable and their internal affairs are not subjected to interference. It also means that all countries' right to independently choose social systems and development paths should be upheld, and that all countries'

---

[3]   Jane Perlez, "Tribunal Rejects Beijing's Claims in South China Sea," *New York Times*, July 12, 2016.

endeavors to promote economic and social development and improve their people's lives should be respected.[4]

For decades, China's leaders have prioritized economic development and avoided burdensome international obligations and war. To reassure countries that are nervous about China's growing power, Beijing has emphasized the country's "peaceful development" for years.[5] Reflecting the country's changing needs as a great power, however, leaders have increasingly discussed how the nation's revitalization, which Xi has called the "China Dream," depends partly on the country's ability to shape a favorable international environment.[6] In the 2015 speech to the UN General Assembly, Xi stated, "We cannot realize the Chinese dream without a peaceful international environment, a stable international order and the understanding, support, and help from the rest of the world."[7]

In spite of its enormous economy, China's leaders and people perceive China as a developing country, not a developed one.[8] In the past, China has used its identity as a developing country to drag its feet on certain international agreements. For example, China had for years relied on its status as a developing country to oppose limits on carbon emissions to reduce climate change or demands to liberalize its economy.[9] Even though China's leaders still prize stable social and economic development, the calculations and strategy for achieving that growth have changed as China's economy has ascended to the upper ranks of

---

[4]   Xi Jinping, "Working Together to Forge a New Partnership of Win-Win Cooperation and Create a Community of Shared Future for Mankind," speech at the General Debate of the 70th Session of the United Nations General Assembly, New York, September 28, 2015b.

[5]   Information Office of the State Council, 2011.

[6]   "Xi Eyes More Enabling Int'l Environment for China's Peaceful Development," *Xinhua*, November 30, 2014b.

[7]   Xi Jinping, "Full Text from President Xi Jinping's Speech," New York City, National Committee on United States-China Relations, September 2015a.

[8]   Matt Ferchen, "The Contradictions of China's Developing Country Identity," Carnegie-Tsinghua Center for Global Policy, June 13, 2014.

[9]   C. Fred Bergsten, "A Partnership of Equals: How Washington Should Respond to China's Economic Challenge," *Foreign Affairs*, June 1, 2008.

world economies. Aware that many countries are more dependent on China's economy than vice versa, China's leaders today might be more willing to take economic risks and even use their economic leverage to pursue national security interests than previous administrations.[10]

Chinese efforts to bolster control of its security interests, even when they overlap with those of neighboring countries, has intensified U.S. anxiety about China's intentions with respect to the existing international order. Citing China's military and paramilitary actions in the East and South China Seas in pursuit of its maritime and territorial claims, some U.S. observers have argued that the PRC has become more "assertive" in its foreign policy—that is, more willing to punish other actors for behaving in ways that threaten China's interests—since 2008.[11] Most U.S. analysts agree that, since around 2009, the PRC has taken more proactive measures to assert control of disputed areas and reacted more abrasively to the actions of its rivals in the same areas, compared with its behavior in the 20 years or so preceding that time.[12]

Increasing Chinese assertiveness starting around 2010 likely developed in response to a combination of external and internal factors. In 2008 and 2009, U.S. preoccupation with the global financial crisis and wars in the Middle East may have led China's leaders to believe that they had more freedom to pursue their claims with impunity. Similarly, Japan's decision to nationalize ownership of the Senkaku Islands likely spurred China to step up its efforts to control the islands. More broadly, China's own perspective is that its actions have been far more defensive and reactive than the image portrayed in the United States. In the ten years after the 2002 Declaration on the Conduct of Parties, designed to moderate disputes over claims, Beijing believes that other claimants, including Vietnam, Malaysia, and the Philippines, "breached the spirit of the document by complicating

---

[10]   William J. Norris, *Chinese Economic Statecraft: Commercial Actors, Grand Strategy, and State Control*, Ithaca, N.Y.: Cornell University Press, 2016, pp. 44–66.

[11]   For a summary of these arguments, see Michael D. Swaine, "Perceptions of an Assertive China," *China Leadership Monitor*, No. 32, May 2010.

[12]   Alastair Iain Johnston, "How New and Assertive Is China's New Assertiveness?" *International Security*, Vol. 37, No. 4, Spring 2013, pp. 19–20.

and escalating disputes."[13] Recent assertiveness, in the view of Chinese officials, is only a delayed reaction to years of provocations. Domestically, nationalism and bureaucratic politics also may have contributed to more hard-line behavior in the South China Sea.[14] Chinese growing economic and military capability, stemming from years of rapid economic growth, may have also emboldened leaders to pursue more assertive policies.

Xi Jinping's Report at the 19th Party Congress

The 19th Party Congress report provides the most recent, comprehensive statement of the strategic and policy directives issued by China's top leadership. Held in 2017, the report's contents carry directives that suggest both support for the international system and an increasing focus on expanding China's influence within the system.[15] On the one hand, the report emphasized China's support for the international system and the authority of the UN. The 19th Party Congress report stated that China will "continue its efforts to safeguard world peace, contribute to global development, and uphold international order." It also affirmed the country's intention to maintain peaceful, cooperative relations with other countries. However, the report also outlined ambitions for the country to become a global leading power. It stated that by mid-century, China seeks to "become a global leader in terms of composite national strength and international influence." Underscoring the country's ambivalence to many aspects of the existing order, it stated that China will "take an active part in reforming and developing

---

[13]   Feng Zhang, "Chinese Thinking on the South China Sea and the Future of Regional Security," *Political Science Quarterly*, Vol. 132, No. 3, 2017, p. 438.

[14]   Andrew Scobell and Scott W. Harold, "An 'Assertive' China? Insights from Interviews," *Asian Security*, Vol. 9, No. 2, 2013, pp. 111–112.

[15]   Xi Jinping, "Secure a Decisive Victory in Building a Moderately Prosperous Society in All Respects and Strive for the Great Success of Socialism with Chinese Characteristics for a New Era," speech to the 19th National Congress of the Communist Party of China, October 18, 2017. The full text has been published in a number of places; we referenced an initial, quasi-official translation. The quotes here come from pp. 9–10, 19, 22, and 26 of this version.

the global governance system, and keep contributing Chinese wisdom and strength to global governance." It also hinted that China intends to build a network of supportive countries around the world, based principally among the developing world.

The report also stated that China intends to seek "partnerships, not alliances," which a commentary on the 19th Congress, published in the *People's Daily*, the official newspaper of the CCP, explained meant that China sought to "form a *global partnership network*" (emphasis ours).[16] Chinese sources depict partnerships as highly moralistic relationships in which China bestows financial and other benefits as the higher-status partner and in return expects deference and cooperation on sensitive issues. As the 19th Party Congress report stated, China will "uphold justice while pursuing shared interests with other countries."[17] Partnerships will be especially critical to facilitating China's ambition to build the Belt and Road Initiative, which the 19th Party Congress highlighted as a priority for years to come. It stated that China intends to build "policy, infrastructure, trade, financial, and people-to-people connectivity," which it said would result in a "new platform for international cooperation to create new drivers of shared development."

In regard to the ways in which China's interests align with a shared order, the speech again reaffirmed well-established themes. Xi pointed proudly to China's regional and global diplomacy conducted through multilateral fora, such as the UN; the Group of Twenty (G-20); the Asian-Pacific Economic Cooperation (APEC) Economic Leaders Meetings; the Brazil, Russia, India, China, and South Africa (BRICS) Summit; and others. It promised that China would lead on global environmental issues, promote globalization, and "develop an open economy." The Chinese Dream, Xi insisted, "can be realized only in a peaceful international environment and under a stable international order." In the process of becoming the fully developed nation of

---

[16] Zhong Sheng, "Significance of 19th CPC Congress, Promoting Community of Common Destiny," Beijing Renmin Ribao Online, November 24, 2017, p. 3.

[17] "Full Text of Xi Jinping's Report to the 19th Party Congress," *Xinhua*, November 3, 2017.

the future, Xi said, China will "become a proud and active member of the community of nations."[18]

The speech also confirmed the accelerating sense of rising power among Chinese leaders and officials, and it hinted at the complications this may pose for the future of China's integration in a truly shared order. Xi boasted that China had now "crossed the threshold into a new era," which represented a "historic juncture in China's development." China had now "achieved a tremendous transformation—it has stood up, grown rich, and become strong; and it now embraces the brilliant prospects of rejuvenation." Such confidence is clearly breeding a desire in China to become more influential in setting and enforcing rules and shaping the character of international politics. (The emerging era, Xi said, will be one "that sees China moving closer to center stage.") The speech was full of references to the steps China is taking to empower and use this new influence, including muscular comments about its growing military capabilities. Whether such ambitions can be aligned with a multilateral order remains unclear. The speech also stressed that China's path offered an example and opportunity for other developing nations—implying that Beijing intends to offer a unique Chinese path to socioeconomic order and development, which could compete with the neoliberal model that has been the basis for the postwar order.

Differing Views of China's Intentions

China's more-assertive behavior reveals a major source of divergence with the United States and its allies regarding the international order. China's coercive seizure of Scarborough Reef in 2012, deployment of the Haiyang oil rig in Vietnam's exclusive economic zone (EEZ) in 2014, and provocative behavior near the Senkaku Islands have ignited a debate among observers regarding China's stance toward the international order. In particular, a significant debate is under way between two broad camps—those who believe that China's growing power and cultural self-confidence are encouraging a dangerous bellicosity that is

---

[18] "Full Text of Xi Jinping's Report to the 19th Party Congress," 2017.

hostile to a rules-based order and those who contend that China is willing to constrain its actions to guarantee a rules-based order, albeit one in which it plays a larger role in determining those rules.[19]

Those who hold a more-hawkish policy toward China tend to regard Beijing as acting in a manner contrary to the international order. These observers tend to characterize the international order more expansively to include not just the formal organizations but also the informal values, institutions, and alliances that underpin Western dominance of the order and underwrite a forceful assertion of liberal values. These observers criticize China for adhering only to the formal institutions while rejecting the informal aspects and liberal norms. They highlight Chinese policy in Asia, in particular, as seeking to provide advantages to Beijing at the expense of the existing order, citing as examples the establishment of the AIIB, Chinese growing criticism of U.S. alliances in the region, and the proposed Belt and Road Initiative. Indeed, some worry that China may be seeking to use such initiatives to build an economic sphere of influence.[20]

By contrast, those who take a more-sanguine view see China as misunderstood and of limited influence. They tend to emphasize the ways in which China's policy aligns with the international order. They argue that concepts of "the order" need to distinguish between the formal aspects that make up the order—which, in their view, China upholds—and the norms, values, and security relationships preferred by the United States. This perspective argues for a more-limited view of the international order that does not include military alliances or privilege Western liberal values. These observers acknowledge that China's policies could challenge U.S. objectives, but they argue that China does not seek to undermine global governance as it currently exists.

As this debate reveals, an important distinction lies in the aspects of the order that reflect U.S. values and interests and those that do not align as closely with U.S. interests. China might be challenging

---

[19] Zhang's "Chinese Thinking on the South China Sea" (2017) contains an excellent summary of differing schools of thought on foreign policy in China today.

[20] Nadège Rolland, "China's 'Belt and Road Initiative': Underwhelming or Game-Changer?" *Washington Quarterly*, Vol. 40, No. 1, Spring 2017, p. 134.

aspects of U.S. dominance or preferences in some cases, but that does not make China hostile to the order as a whole. Studies of China's UN voting relative to the United States, for example, may be misleading; even if there is a growing divergence, this may account for growing rivalry between the two states rather than rising Chinese challenges to "the order." Indeed, China's UN voting behavior relative to other states perceived as leading sponsors of the liberal order, such as Britain and Sweden, does not appear to show a marked change in recent years.[21]

China unsurprisingly favors those institutions, such as the UN, that reflect more independent, value-neutral expressions of the international order. In some cases, such as nonproliferation, China has been willing to cooperate with the United States to enforce norms. However, in general, China remains wary of those aspects of the international order that most closely align with U.S. values and interests, such as human rights, military alliances, and liberal democratic values.

This tension emerges especially in regard to U.S.-led security alliances and institutions. While the United States and its allies describe these commitments as part of the liberal international order, China (and some others) perceive them as nothing more than bilateral and multilateral U.S. security policies. Many officials throughout the Asia-Pacific region, for example, consider the U.S. security ties to South Korea and Japan as centerpieces of the postwar international order. Many analysts, even some in China, recognize the stabilizing influence of these relationships. However, Chinese authorities have increasingly voiced criticism of the alliances as destabilizing and threatening, especially in Asia.[22] Despite the criticism, China remains convinced that aggressive efforts to oppose the United States would be counterproductive and would only isolate China.[23] Balancing the desire to coun-

---

[21] See, for example, Peter Ferdinand, "Rising Powers at the UN: An Analysis of the Voting Behavior of BRICS in the General Assembly," *Third World Quarterly*, Vol. 35, No. 3, 2014.

[22] Timothy R. Heath, "China and the U.S. Alliance System," *The Diplomat*, July 11, 2014a; Adam P. Liff, "China and the U.S. Alliance System," *The China Quarterly*, Vol. 233, April 2017, pp. 137–165.

[23] Yong Deng, "Hegemon on the Offensive: Chinese Perspectives on U. S. Global Strategy," *Political Science Quarterly*, Vol. 116, No. 3, 2001, p. 362.

ter U.S. influence in Asia with the imperative to avoid a debilitating war, China has opted instead to erode U.S. influence through gradual measures.

In sum, it can be difficult to identify what counts as a "challenge" to the order because of the overlap between the informal aspects that align with U.S. values and interests and the formal aspects that are more independent of U.S. power. In some cases, key international accords that China refuses to sign, such as the International Criminal Court, are the same ones that the United States has rejected, often for the same reason—concern for sovereignty.

CHAPTER THREE

China's Views of International Order

China's national interests provide the basis for its view of the postwar international order. In its official documents and strategies, statements of senior leaders, and analysis by unofficial but government-affiliated scholars and institutes, China has outlined a wealth of views on the postwar order.[1]

In the Maoist era, Chinese leaders cultivated relations with the developing world and with either the Soviet Union or the United States, as the situation warranted. Because of China's poverty and political isolation, Chinese leaders in the Mao era interacted little with the UN and other major institutions of the international system. However, China's diplomatic thought and actions changed significantly following U.S. recognition and the advent of reform and opening-up policies in the late 1970s. China entered the UN, expanded its role in international trade, and took greater interest in international developments.

Today, China's leaders appreciate the legitimacy embodied in equitable institutions and fair rules and decisionmaking processes, as well as the flexibility of an order that allows Beijing to exert influence. However, Chinese leaders resent what they regard as disproportionate benefits that the United States receives from existing institutions.[2] They also resist international norms, institutions, and decisions that

---

[1] For a survey of China's changing view of and engagement with international institutions, see Marc Lanteigne, *China and International Institutions: Alternate Paths to Global Power*, London: Routledge, 2005.

[2] Fu Ying, "China and the Future of the International Order," London, speech at Chatham House, July 6, 2016a.

they regard as privileging Western countries and threatening to the importance placed on national sovereignty favored by China and many developing countries.

In general, when Chinese authorities insist that the country "supports the international order," they are typically referring to China's participation in the established organizations and institutions, such as the UN and the WTO, and its support for many international laws and treaties.[3] By contrast, Chinese leaders and thinkers criticize the liberal norms and values that buttress the international order as a Western "political ideology." A scholar at the Ministry of State Security's Chinese Institute for Contemporary International Relations (CICIR), Niu Xinchun, explained that China had "integrated successfully into the international economic system" but noted "increasing difficulties with political and ideological integration." He described the political ideology underpinning the international order as a Western one that is poorly suited to the needs of rising powers. For example, he contrasted what he deemed the West's preference for "hegemony" with what he assessed to be a preference among non-Western countries for a "balance of power," "capitalism" with "socialism" and other economic models, and "democracy" with "authoritarianism" and other modes of government. Reflecting a suspicion widespread in Chinese media commentary and academic writings, Niu accused the United States of attempting to "incorporate and tame China" through its Western political ideology.[4]

Within that general context, we find a number of broad themes in China's official statements about international order.[5]

---

[3] "China Supports, Contributes to Postwar International Order," *Xinhua*, July 30, 2015.

[4] Niu Xinchun, "U.S.-China Relations: Collision and Competition of Ideologies," *Research in International Problems* [国际问题研究], March 13, 2012, pp. 78–89.

[5] Thomas J. Christensen, *The China Challenge: Shaping the Choices of a Rising Power*, New York: W. W. Norton, 2016, pp. 20–25, 39–40.

Support for Institutions That Grant China Influence

First, China's leaders express support for international institutions that grant China significant influence or, at minimum, influence equal to that of other countries. In the UN, for example, China is granted veto power as a permanent member of the Security Council, which it has exercised occasionally.[6] In the WTO, all members, including China, have an equal vote and ability to initiate the dispute resolution process. In institutions in which China has less influence, however, China's leaders want the allocation of decisionmaking power to be redistributed so that China has a greater voice in determining outcomes. For example, for many years, China petitioned for the Chinese currency, the renminbi, to be included as one of the international reserve currencies included in the IMF's Special Drawing Right (SDR). In 2016, after meeting the IMF's standards, the renminbi became the first currency added to the SDR list in 15 years.[7] Where institutional reform in line with China's interests has not been forthcoming or has seemed unlikely, China has begun building international or regional institutions in which it has a leading role.[8] This is particularly true within its immediate geographic region, where China has created institutions such as the Shanghai Cooperation Organization (SCO)—a security-based forum with Russia and states in Central Asia—and the AIIB, the China Association of Southeast Asian Nations (ASEAN) Free Trade Area (CAFTA), and others. In these institutions, China's leaders have greater influence over setting the agenda, which could better enable them to use these institutions to achieve national goals.

China's search for influence and status through its participation in the international order is an important factor shaping its preferences. "In general," the scholar Ann Kent argues, "it now prefers to be seen

---

6   Security Council Report, *The Security Council Veto*, New York: United Nations Security Council, December 2016.

7   IMF, "IMF Survey: Chinese Renminbi to Be Included in IMF's Special Drawing Right Basket," December 1, 2015; David Francis, "IMF Officially Gives China Seat at the Adult Table of World Economics," *Foreign Policy*, October 3, 2016.

8   Daniel McDowell, "New Order: China's Challenge to the Global Financial System," *World Politics Review*, April 14, 2015.

as part of a global consensus rather than as a spoiler of international harmony."[9] It reflects a larger argument of this study about the value of a generally recognized multilateral order: It becomes the normative and rule-based standard against which state actions are judged. At least so far, and in powerful ways as recently as 2017, the Chinese government has signaled a desire to seek influence and status mostly by being viewed as a responsible leader of a multilateral order—rather than, for example, acquiring such unilateral power that it can simply dictate outcomes and ignore multilateral considerations, rules, and norms.

The distinction China draws is between a "multipolar" order— i.e., one in which non-Western countries have a more equally weighted say in setting norms and making decisions within international institutions—and the current order, which China regards as a largely "unipolar" one that privileges the United States and its allies. One of the reasons China's leaders offer for reforming representation within existing international institutions is their belief that the distribution of global power is shifting as emerging markets and developing countries rise.[10]

Chinese principles appear to have their own contradictions, however. China has, for example, proven reluctant to support an expanded role for other major non-Western countries that it views as competitors, such as India and Japan. In 2005, China—along with the United States—vetoed a proposal to enlarge the UN Security Council by adding six permanent members, which would most likely have included Japan, Germany, India, and Brazil (the proposal's sponsors).[11] While China favors a version of multipolarity that reduces U.S. predominance, it also expects to gain its own degree of regional predominance—making for a highly constrained, Sinocentric version of a multipolar order, at least within Asia.

---

[9]   Ann Kent, "China's International Socialization: The Role of International Organizations," *Global Governance*, Vol. 8, No. 3, July–September 2002, pp. 343–344, 349, 358.

[10]   Xi, 2015b.

[11]   "Washington, Beijing Agree to Block G4 Plan," *Xinhua*, August 4, 2005.

Appreciation for Rules-Based, Multilateral Mechanisms

Second, in general, China's leaders express appreciation for the fact that the international order is based on rules and multilateral decisionmaking mechanisms, which bring stability, predictability, and legitimacy to state behavior and international relations.[12] They particularly value the UN's role as a forum for multilateral decisions about the use of force. China also has become an active participant in WTO dispute proceedings—both as a complainant and as a respondent. According to the Office of the U.S. Trade Representative, China is compliant with WTO regulations in most areas and has on occasion used appropriate dispute resolution mechanisms in the WTO.[13] As of April 2013, 18 cases (out of 30 total cases) brought against China in the WTO had been resolved; China reached mutually agreed solutions in nine cases and fully complied with rulings in eight out of nine cases.[14]

Contestation of Western Values and U.S. Military Power

Third, China contests the aspects of the order that reflect Western values emphasizing human rights and democracy or enhancing U.S. military power. For example, China's leaders argue that U.S. military alliances are not part of the international order. Instead, they view these alliances as part of a plan to "contain" China.[15] Similarly, China's leaders criticize some of the liberal democratic norms embedded in the order, especially when they perceive those norms as in tension with the

---

[12] Thomas Fingar, "China's Vision of World Order," in Ashley J. Tellis and Travis Tanner, eds., *Strategic Asia 2012–2013: China's Military Challenge*, Seattle: National Bureau of Asian Research, 2012, p. 348.

[13] Office of the U.S. Trade Representative, *2015 Report to Congress on China's WTO Compliance*, Washington, D.C., December 2015.

[14] Xiaowen Zhang and Xiaoling Li, "The Politics of Compliance with Adverse WTO Dispute Settlement Rulings in China," *Journal of Contemporary China*, Vol. 23, No. 85, 2014, p. 146.

[15] For a discussion of the containment question, see Shannon Tiezzi, "Yes, the U.S. Does Want to Contain China (Sort Of)," *The Diplomat*, August 8, 2015.

Westphalian sovereignty norms that they believe form the foundation of the order.[16] As former National Security Council Senior Director for Asian Affairs Jeffrey Bader put it, "China often defends the more old-fashioned interpretation of sovereignty against efforts to reinterpret sovereignty in a more limited way."[17] China has been especially critical of areas where liberal democratic values and U.S. military power intersect, such as U.S.-led measures to revise aspects of the international order in favor of military intervention for humanitarian reasons under the "responsibility to protect" norm.[18]

Criticism of U.S. Exceptionalism

Fourth, China's leaders resent the freedom with which the United States acts, especially when U.S. actions violate the order's rules and circumvent the order's decisionmaking mechanisms. For example, they often criticize the United States when it contravenes UN Security Council resolutions, as in the 2003 invasion of Iraq.[19] At the same time, however, China wishes to enjoy the same exceptionalism that the United States applies to itself. When China's interests are best served by violating rules, it has acted unilaterally against the will of international organizations and other countries. In the case of the South China Sea, for example, China denied the Permanent Court of Arbitration's (PCA's) authority to rule on rights afforded by sovereignty claims between the Philippines and China, and it rejected the final PCA ruling, which

---

[16]   Amitai Etzioni and G. John Ikenberry, "Is China More Westphalian Than the West?" *Foreign Affairs*, October 17, 2011.

[17]   Jeffrey A. Bader, "How Xi Jinping Sees the World . . . and Why," *Order from Chaos: Foreign Policy in a Troubled World*, Asia Working Group, Brookings Institution, February 2016, p. 189.

[18]   Zheng Chen, "China and the Responsibility to Protect," *Journal of Contemporary China*, Vol. 25, 2016, pp. 686–700; Christensen, 2016, pp. 25, 59.

[19]   Permanent Mission of the People's Republic of China to the United Nations, "China's Position on the War in Iraq," March 26, 2003.

criticized China's historical "nine-dash line" claim.[20] Recognizing that its leverage in these disputes is greatest in bilateral settings, China has resisted attempts to handle disputes through multilateral legal and consultative processes. Instead, it has engaged in reclamation and militarization of disputed claims in the South China Sea, enhancing its ability to project power around its claims and deter or pressure competing claimants.[21]

Criticism of Military Interventionism

Fifth, Beijing is skeptical of U.S. and European security policies that appeal to such values as individual freedom, democracy, and human rights. Chinese officials have frequently criticized, in particular, military actions and operations that do not have the backing of the UN.[22] A commentary in China's official English-language newspaper, *China Daily*, reflected a disposition commonly encountered in official media when it derided a "Pax Americana" for furthering a "period of incessant warfare" through "Western policies of military intervention and regime change" even as it upheld the authority of the UN.[23] This opposition has become especially pointed after the 2011 operation in Libya, in which hesitant Chinese support for the initial direction of Western policy helped produced dangerous outcomes from Beijing's point of view—military intervention that went well beyond the initial UN mandate.[24]

---

[20] Ministry of Foreign Affairs of the People's Republic of China, "Foreign Ministry Spokesperson Lu Kang's Regular Press Conference of July 13, 2016," webpage, July 13, 2016.

[21] Asia Maritime Transparency Initiative, "China Island Tracker," webpage, Center for Strategic and International Studies, undated. Since 2013, Beijing has reclaimed more than 3,200 miles of land around features in the South China Sea.

[22] "The International Law Ironies of US Provocations in the South China Sea," *Xinhua*, January 31, 2016.

[23] Chua Chin Leng, "The Politics of Non-Interference—A New World Order," *China Daily*, January 25, 2016.

[24] Christensen, 2016, pp. 267–270.

In sum, the evidence suggests three major tensions in China's attitude toward the postwar international order. The first is between its appreciation for the stability and prosperity enabled by the current international order and a desire to use international institutions to help bring about a more equitable distribution of power between the United States and China. A second tension is between the order's increasingly interventionist elements and China's abiding concern with sovereignty.[25] A third and final major tension is between China's commitment to rules at the international level and its own conception for its regional role, which involves a form of preeminence that privileges it with the power to set norms and make exceptions as its interests demand. These dilemmas suggest that the relationship between China and the international order will remain a complex and challenging interaction.

---

[25]   Kent, 2002, p. 358.

CHAPTER FOUR

China's Behavior Toward the Order

After reviewing China's interests and broad attitude toward the postwar international order, we reviewed evidence relating to its actual behavior toward the components of that order. We reviewed data about China's participation in major international institutions, support for international norms, role in informal multilateral organizations and processes, and degree of compliance with the rules and norms of the order.

Although the data were often incomplete or inconclusive, the overall lessons of this analysis were clear. First, the broad trajectory of China's engagement with the order, at least through 2008, was generally supportive of existing institutions. The PRC moved from Maoist revolutionary aspirations regarding the global capitalist system in the 1960s to a posture of joining every major international institution and participating in increasingly active ways.

Second, China's overall involvement in international institutions, as measured by its membership and participation in relevant organizations, has become as significant as just about any major state besides the United States.

Third, as noted earlier, China's behavior has to be disaggregated among various types of order or elements of the postwar order—the economic order, security order, human rights order, and so on. Its behavior has been far more supportive in some areas (such as economics) than others (such as human rights).

Fourth, China's compliance with the essential rules and norms of the order is uneven, especially in areas of human rights and freedom of expression, but it shows many areas of improvement. China's support for institutions and norms, like that of the United States, also includes examples in which it carves out exceptions for itself.

Finally, as in the general Chinese attitudes toward order, in its behavior we find a clear dividing line between actions toward the general multilateral order built on the UN system (which have been more favorable), as opposed to actions toward those components of the order that reflect U.S. predominance, such as the regional alliance system (which have been far more critical and, at times, confrontational).

Chapter Five considers how China's attitude to the order may be changing under the influence of trends in world politics, such as the perceived relative decline of U.S. influence and the acceleration of China's ambitions for regional hegemony. Such trends may prove to be catalysts of a different Chinese attitude toward the international order. This chapter merely surveys evidence to date.

China and International Institutions

An initial indicator of China's behavior toward the postwar order is its degree of participation in the basic institutions that define that order. Broadly speaking, this indicator points to a significant and growing positive Chinese interaction with the order, based on the institutions it has joined and the nature of its role in them.

China's history provides critical context to this analysis. As recently as the 1960s, China remained a revolutionary state, self-consciously determined to undermine and overthrow the U.S.-led global capitalist order. Yet through much of the Cold War, Beijing also portrayed itself as a representative for the developing world through its support for the nonaligned movement. Thus, China's current posture as a self-described leader of globalization and sponsor of a multilateral order represents a dramatic evolution from its position as a poor, developing country three decades ago. That position could change again— but, broadly speaking, China's engagement with the postwar order has unquestionably been on a positive trajectory.

This is reflected first and foremost in China's extensive participation in the formal and informal institutions of the order. As Andrew

Nathan has argued, China has "moved from a position of almost no participation in international regimes to the current position in which it participates in almost all of the major international regimes in which it is eligible to participate."[1] Table 4.1 displays the major institutions that China supports and has actively joined in recent decades.

In a number of particular institutions, China of late has become an active contributor and increasingly powerful voice. This has included UN peacekeeping operations, where China has become the top contributor of troops among the Permanent Five members.[2] China has also

Table 4.1
China's Participation in Major International Institutions

Major International Institutions[a]
• UN
• UN peacekeeping operations
• The WTO
• The WB
• The IMF
• The G-20
• International Labor Organization (ILO)
• APEC
• The International Atomic Energy Agency
• Biological Weapons Convention
• Nuclear Nonproliferation Treaty (NPT)
• Chemical Weapons Convention
• Comprehensive Test Ban Treaty (CTBT)
• UN Environmental Program
• Conference on Disarmament
• Montreal Protocols
• Paris Accord on Climate
• Convention on Rights of Persons with Disabilities
• Anti-Ballistic Missile Treaty (ABMT)

[a] This list includes only major institutions. China is also a member or signatory of hundreds of minor institutions, conventions, treaties, agreements, and committees.

---

[1]   Andrew J. Nathan, "China's Rise and International Regimes: Does China Seek to Overthrow Global Norms?" in Robert S. Ross and Jo Inge Bekkevold, eds., *China in the Era of Xi Jinping: Domestic and Foreign Policy Challenges*, Washington, D.C.: Georgetown University Press, 2016, p. 171.

[2]   Sarah Zheng, "China Completes Registration of 8,000 Strong UN Peace Keeping Force, Defense Ministry Says," *South China Morning Post*, September 29, 2017. For a general dis-

trained UN troops and has sought to place officials into top UN jobs.[3] It has become a leader of the global climate response and an increasingly powerful voice on proliferation issues in North Korea.

China's engagement with the institutions of the order is not comprehensive or without exceptions. It has rejected or refused to participate in several. However, so has the United States—and, in many cases, the United States and China are shunning the same institutions. Table 4.2 indicates the major institutions of the order that have been either rejected, or accepted only with great qualification, by China and the United States. As the table makes clear, there is significant overlap between the two countries' exceptions.

Broadly speaking, China's active participation has tended to reflect its general views of order, in particular its emphasis on the essential sovereignty guarantees of the UN Charter and the multilateral spirit of the broader UN system.[4] Its participation has been less consistent in areas

Table 4.2
Opposition to International Institutions—China and the United States

China	United States
• Rome Statute (establishing the International Criminal Court) • Land Mines Convention • Proliferation Security Initiative • Economic sanctions processes not ratified by UN Security Council • International Court of Justice jurisdiction over sovereignty issues	• Rome Statute (establishing the International Criminal Court) • Land Mines Convention • International Court of Justice jurisdiction over sovereignty issues

SOURCES: These examples are derived from Nathan, 2016, pp. 171–172, and the figures in Johnston, 2015.

---

cussion of China's peacekeeping role, see Christensen, 2016, pp. 161–165, 233–240, and 266–270; and Evan S. Medeiros, *China's International Behavior: Activism, Opportunism, and Diversification*, Santa Monica, Calif.: RAND Corporation, MG-850-AF, 2009.

[3]   Colum Lynch, "China Eyes Ending Western Grip on Top UN Jobs with Greater Control Over Blue Helmets," *Foreign Policy*, October 2, 2016.

[4]   Gregory Chin and Ramesh Thakur, "Will China Change the Rules of Global Order?" *Washington Quarterly*, Vol. 33, No. 4, October 2010, pp. 128–129; G. John Ikenberry and Darren Lim, "China's Emerging Institutional Statecraft," Brookings Institution, April 2017;

of perceived U.S. hegemony or liberal value promotion. In this sense, as noted earlier, its engagement with the order as a whole is much more positive in several suborders—economics; social and political development; the UN order based on sovereignty; and elements of the security order, including nonproliferation, counterterrorism, and counterpiracy.[5] China has, however, stepped up its involvement in conflict mediation in central Asia and Africa. It has, for example, sponsored talks between feuding factions in Afghanistan and promoted peace talks between warring groups in Sudan.[6]

One complication in using simple membership as an indicator is that formal votes and other measurable signals of participation in the order do not always convey significant modes of influence or normative changes. Equally important, if not more so, is the nuance of what occurs between votes—the persuasion, compromise, advocacy of interests, and other dialogues that happen behind the scenes. The compromises and consensus worked out behind the scenes before final decisions are made are considered most important in such institutions as the UN and WTO. It is increasingly important to have China on board when making global decisions. Beijing uses this reality to China's advantage.

Arguably the biggest risks to the international order from China would come not from its obvious, quantifiable engagement with the order but from its subtle, qualitative moves: China could be working within the order while simultaneously exercising a quiet, contrarian influence that would be difficult to detect and could be destabilizing in the long term. China is the second largest economy in the WTO and the head of the International Telecommunication Union; these are the places where we should be looking for China to challenge the system. Even China's creation of alternate institutions (such as the AIIB) is in

---

Stephen Olson and Clyde Prestowitz, "The Evolving Role of China in International Institutions," U.S. China Economic and Security Review Commission, January 2011.

[5]   Johnston, 2016, pp. 7–17.

[6]   Edward Wong and David Jolly, "China Considers Larger Role in Afghan Peace Process," *New York Times*, January 24, 2016; International Crisis Group, "China's Foreign Policy Experiment in South Sudan," Report No. 288, July 10, 2017.

part about gaining the leverage it needs to increase its power within existing institutions (such as the WB and IMF).

Another important theme is China's growing role in regional institutions.[7] In its engagement with ASEAN and its multiple subgroupings, as well as its role in such China-sponsored regional organizations as the Regional Comprehensive Economic Partnership (RCEP), Beijing has pursued a multitrack strategy of serving its essential interests. On the one hand, it has sought significant interaction with regional institutions and used its participation to project an image of peaceful coexistence, hoping to ease regional fears of China's looming power. On the other hand, it has sought unquestioned predominance in these institutions, reflecting its general view of itself as the natural regional hegemon. In these relationships, China is pressing the limits of multilateral equity, demanding that others defer to it as the regionally preeminent power. It is a consistent theme—participating in international institutions but shaping them to better support China's interests and ambitions.[8]

To be sure, China has increasingly flexed its muscles within international institutions to achieve self-interested reforms. In this sense, China's behavior has not been characterized by a simple joining of existing institutions but rather by participation followed by gradual efforts to gain support for a Chinese model of how such institutions can and should work.[9]

In this regard, China's behavior in international economic forums offers an example of its general posture. In these settings, China has evolved to become what could be described as a "selective revisionist," looking to promote its own economic interests through exceptions and

---

[7]   Claudia Astartia, "China's Role in Southeast Asian Regional Organizations," *China Perspectives*, Vol. 3, 2008; Paul De Grauwe and Zhaoyong Zhang, "The Rise of China and Regional Integration in East Asia," *Scottish Journal of Political Economy*, Vol. 63, No. 1, 2016; Ellen Frost, "China's Activities in Southeast Asia and the Implications for U.S. Interests—Panel V: China and Regional Forums," Washington, D.C., testimony before the U.S.-China Economic and Security Review Commission, February 4, 2010.

[8]   Yuen Foong Khong, "Primacy or World Order? The United States and China's Rise—A Review Essay," *International Security*, Vol. 38, No. 3, Winter 2013–2014, pp. 161–164.

[9]   Nathan, 2016, p. 189.

special conditions for China.[10] There is a growing worry that China may not be internalizing the principle of reciprocity—that its zero-sum mindset leads it to seek uneven trade terms at every opportunity. However, China participates actively in the WTO and is a leading user of the dispute resolution mechanism; it appears to largely abide by direct rulings of the WTO, and it has undertaken extensive domestic reforms to meet conditions imposed by the WTO, IMF, and WB.

Finally, China's role in international institutions reflects general limits on the decisiveness of its foreign policy generally. At least until recently, China has been more of a free-rider in the institutions of the order than an active investor and contributor.[11] It often expressed its voice in behind-the-scenes ways and seldom led on issues in a very public way. The 19th Party Congress provided evidence that China's leadership intends to step up the country's global leadership role in coming years, however. In that report, the country's highest-level document containing strategic directives, Chinese leaders outlined the ambition for the country to have "become a global leader in terms of composite national strength and international influence" by mid-century. The report called for expanding China's network of partner countries around the world and highlighted major geostrategic initiatives, such as the Belt and Road Initiative.[12]

China and International Norms

Apart from participation in formal institutions, China's behavior toward the order can also be assessed relative to its adherence to leading norms. For the purposes of this analysis, we have identified three

---

[10] For a detailed analysis of this approach in terms of international financial institutions, see Daniel McDowell, "New Order: China's Challenge to the Global Financial System," *World Politics Review*, April 14, 2015.

[11] Bree Feng, "Obama's 'Free Rider' Comment Draws Chinese Criticism," *New York Times*, August 13, 2014.

[12] "Full Text of Xi Jinping's Report to the 19th Party Congress," 2017.

norm sets to judge Chinese behavior: human rights, nonproliferation, and nonaggression.

It is in the area of human rights—and, more broadly, the distinctly liberal elements of the postwar order—that China's behavior most clearly contradicts the order. It has joined most human rights conventions and regimes, but its behavior within them has been hypocritical and instrumental.[13] It has sought to weaken enforcement while still portraying itself as a responsible member of the international community through its participation in the covenants. Its position on such norms, even on economic openness, leaves China somewhat handicapped as a potential leader of a globalizing order.[14] Recent trends in press freedom, public debate, crackdowns on dissent, and emphasis on ideological indoctrination have been starkly negative.[15]

Until recently, however, the trajectory of China's engagement with the international human rights regime—while still primarily defensive and, in many ways, contradictory—has been at least somewhat positive, with Beijing acceding to most major global human rights conventions and offering lip service to their inherent norms. While limited, such actions constitute an important step toward more legitimate reflection of those norms. In its international actions, moreover, China has joined other major powers in opposing cases of unambiguous genocide or ethnic cleansing. Finally, some of the normative exceptions that China has carved out overlap with exceptions claimed by the United States. Both reject the international norm that views the death penalty as a human rights violation, for example, and both have opposed the

---

[13] Nathan, 2016, p. 174. For more specific examples of China's behavior, see Sonya Sceats and Shaun Breslin, "China and the International Human Rights System," Chatham House Report, October 2012; and Chen Dingding, "China's Participation in the International Human Rights Regime: A State Identity Perspective," *Chinese Journal of International Politics*, Vol. 2, No. 3, July 2009. For the most recent assessment of human rights trends within China, see Human Rights Watch, *World Report 2017, Events of 2016: China*, New York, 2017.

[14] Elizabeth C. Economy, "Beijing Is No Champion of Globalization," *Foreign Affairs*, January 22, 2017.

[15] Associated Press, "Human Rights in China Under Xi Worst Since Tiananmen: Amnesty," *South China Morning Post*, November 17, 2017.

International Criminal Court as a transgression of state sovereignty. China has also stepped up its involvement in providing disaster relief and humanitarian assistance, as well as leading mediation efforts in some countries, such as Sudan.

However, under President Xi, China's views of human rights have grown more critical as its government has intensified a political crackdown. Trends in recent years have been uniformly negative, with Beijing undertaking numerous means of constraining basic freedoms and harassing perceived opponents of the CCP, both at home and abroad. At the same time, the government is investing in a range of new technologies and capabilities, such as persistent video surveillance and facial recognition, designed in part to provide even more intrusive means of social control. Measured by its own domestic behavior, therefore, China's behavior has become increasingly opposed to the liberal norms of the postwar order. This trend looks likely to continue in the medium-term future, increasingly powered by the deployment of a range of Orwellian technologies that provide an authoritarian government with an unprecedented ability to monitor social activity.

In another area, nonproliferation, the trajectory of China's integration with international norms has been significantly more positive than in the area of human rights.[16] Beijing has shown gradual improvement in support for the rules and norms of the global nonproliferation regime.[17] In that and related areas of security and arms control, such

---

[16] See Christensen, 2016, pp. 120–137, 185–189, 222–233, and 270–278.

[17] Katherine Combes, "Between Revisionism and Status Quo: China in International Regimes," *Polis*, Vol. 6, Winter 2011–2012, pp. 24–29; Wendy Frieman, *China, Arms Control and Nonproliferation*, London: Routledge, 2004; Shirley Kan, *China and Proliferation of Weapons of Mass Destruction and Missiles: Policy Issues*, Washington, D.C.: Congressional Research Service, RL31555, January 5, 2015; Xia Liping, "Nuclear Nonproliferation from a Chinese Perspective," Bonn, Germany: *Friedrich Ebert Stiftung*, Shanghai Briefing Paper No. 8, 2008; Mohiaddin Mesbahi and Mohammed Homayounvash, "China and the International Nonproliferation Regime: The Case of Iran," *Sociology of Islam*, Vol. 4, No. 1–2, 2016; and Nicola Horsburgh, *China and Global Nuclear Order: From Estrangement to Active Engagement*, Cambridge, UK: Cambridge University Press, 2015.

as the CTBT and ABMT, China has sought to strengthen these areas' legitimacy.[18]

Even here, as in all areas, there is evidence of contradictions and some degree of hypocrisy in China's approach.[19] In its export and arms sales policies, China has often circumvented the spirit and sometimes the letter of nonproliferation regimes. It supported Pakistan's nuclear ambitions, and Chinese nationals have reportedly been involved in providing military and nuclear technology to Iran.[20] The pattern has been similar in some ways to the human rights regime: formal commitment to regimes followed by uneven compliance.[21] Its support for international nonproliferation efforts has also reflected China's interests as much or more than a devotion to the purity of nonproliferation of norms—a pattern that emerged in the recent Iranian nuclear negotiations, in which China reportedly advocated for weaker sanctions standards and enforcement criteria in part to safeguard the interests of Chinese business.[22]

Finally, the UN Charter and many regional treaties and conventions enshrine what may be the single most defining norm of the postwar order—a prohibition on unprovoked territorial aggression. China has repeatedly asserted its support for strict interpretations of sovereignty and norms of nonintervention and nonaggression. China has also rejected outside efforts to influence its political trajectory. In its actual behavior, however, China has—like many other major powers—diverged from a strict interpretation in this area of norms. Especially in threats against Taiwan and its assertion of territorial claims in the East

---

[18]   Kent, 2002, p. 355.

[19]   J. Mohan Malik, "China and the Nuclear Non-Proliferation Regime," *Contemporary Southeast Asia*, Vol. 22, No. 3, 2000.

[20]   Andrew Small, "How China Helped Pakistan Build the Bomb," *The Telegraph*, November 15, 2015; Bernt Berger and Philip Schell, "Toeing the Line, Drawing the Line: China and Iran's Nuclear Ambitions," *China Report*, Vol. 49, No. 1, 2013.

[21]   Ian J. Stewart, "China and Non-Proliferation: Progress at Last?" *The Diplomat*, March 25, 2015.

[22]   Roncevert Ganon Almond, "China and the Iran Nuclear Deal," *The Diplomat*, March 8, 2016.

and South China Seas, China has engaged in conduct that many states have interpreted as interstate coercion, although China has justified its actions as defensive measures to shore up long-standing sovereignty claims. Its support for sovereignty is arguably merely instrumental and designed to support its own interests, rather than a socialized adherence to a clear norm.[23]

It has done so, however, in mostly gradual and restrained ways that have not crossed the threshold into outright interstate aggression. China has sought to establish a distinction between the gray zone coercion in the South and East China Seas and more traditional types of interstate aggression, which are the focus of the UN Charter and related regional agreements. Many observers have characterized these as forms of aggression—and, in many ways, they are, especially in their most bellicose form, such as the forcible seizure of Scarborough Shoals. However, for the most part, the intent of these tactics is to remain *below* the threshold of overt territorial aggression—to continue respecting at least the letter of that law while promoting China's claims.

Even here, however, the pattern has been mixed and does not represent a consistent pattern of aggression. Since the 1990s, China has undertaken a series of regional territorial claims and other interests, but these have typically provoked significant regional reaction and provoked cooling-off periods in which China has undertaken fence-mending diplomatic initiatives. Some of these efforts have led to active engagement with regional conflict resolution processes, including, most recently, senior meetings of the ASEAN group in 2016 and 2017 in which China endorsed negotiations for a code of conduct for regional activities and expressed a hope for negotiated settlements. One analysis of its economic diplomacy in the region suggests that it has not actually moved to punish other claimants in the South China Sea context as much as commonly assumed.[24]

---

[23] Ryan Griffiths, "The Future of Self-Determination and Territorial Integrity in the Asian Century," *Pacific Review*, Vol. 27, No. 3, 2014, p. 466–469.

[24] Angela Poh, "The Myth of Chinese Sanctions over South China Sea Disputes," *Washington Quarterly*, Vol. 40, No. 1, Spring 2017.

Most fundamentally, in China's view, it is *responding* to aggressive actions and claims from other states at least as much as it is initiating or intensifying its own claims. Some analysts have termed the country's policy as "reactive assertiveness," suggesting that Beijing's fundamental impulse is to respond vigorously to others' actions, while others invoke the term to suggest that China seeks pretexts to carry out planned actions.[25] If we measure China's behavior toward the territorial norms of the order *to date*, then—in particular, if we limit the period to the past two or three decades—the record does not yet include significant examples of outright norm violations as much as pushing the boundaries of international law, responding to perceived actions by others, and laying the groundwork for future actions.

If we are to assess China's respect for the norm of nonaggression, therefore, we must have a sense of what that term means. Amitai Etzioni has recommended a definition limited to the use of force,[26] and this comes closest to the specific norm upheld by the UN Charter. We might add that norm-prohibited aggression is generally focused on violations of territorial integrity.[27] The nonaggression norm, then, refers specifically to outright interstate aggression.

There are various ways to assess China's adherence to this narrower interpretation of the nonaggression norm. One is to assess China's history as an initiator of militarized interstate disputes (MIDs). These data are complex and open to various interpretations. The outcomes could reflect various factors—some states have more global reach and more intensely perceived global interests than others, for example, and therefore simply have more inherent capability to become involved in disputes. Involvement in MIDs does not imply militaristic revisionism: As Table 4.3 indicates, the United States typically shows up toward the

---

[25] See, for example, Wei Zongyou, "China's Maritime Trap," *Washington Quarterly*, Vol. 40, No. 1, Spring 2017, pp. 171–173.

[26] Amitai Etzioni, "How Aggressive Is China?" *Korean Journal of International Studies*, Vol. 14, No. 2, August 2016.

[27] Mark W. Zacher, "The Territorial Integrity Norm: International Boundaries and the Use of Force," *International Organization*, Vol. 55, No. 2, 2001.

Table 4.3
**States Initiating Militarized Interstate Disputes,
1990–2010**

State	Number of MIDs Initiated
Russia	48
United States	43
Turkey	35
China	33
Iran	29
Ethiopia	17
Israel	17
India	15

SOURCE: Correlates of War Project, undated-a.

top of lists of states that engage in the most MIDs. Nonetheless, the data can offer some sense of a state's general security behavior.

One early theme in using these data to evaluate Chinese actions, proposed by Alastair Iain Johnston and others, was that the data suggested that China acted to sustain perceived identity and status flaws and that as its power grew it would be less likely to engage in MIDs.[28] A more recent review of the data argues instead that China has not become a satisfied power and instead remains "dispute-prone" and likely to engage in MIDs, especially as its power allows it to pursue policy goals through force.[29] A shortcoming with the data is that they were best catalogued through 2010 as part of the Correlates of War Project[30]—and, in fact, most events come from periods when China was governed by a radically different sort of regime.

[28] Alastair Iain Johnston, "China's Militarized Interstate Dispute Behavior, 1949–1992: A First Cut at the Data," *China Quarterly*, No. 153, 1998.

[29] John J. Chin, "China's Militarized Interstate Dispute Behavior, 1949–2001: A Second Cut at the Data," unpublished manuscript, March 11, 2013.

[30] The data are available online (Correlates of War Project, homepage, undated-a).

Our own analysis of the Correlates of War data shows China as the initiator of 98 MIDs since 1945. This is a significant number but fewer than Russia (143), the United States (113), and Iran (103). Iran and Turkey, each with much smaller regional profiles and more constrained interests than China, each initiated more than 60 MIDs during this time period. Perhaps more significant is the number of MIDs initiated in the post–Cold War period, reflected in Table 4.3. This suggests that China has not been unusually aggressive relative to the pattern of many states with significant global or regional interests.[31] On the other hand, this is not a portrait of a completely satisfied state taking no aggressive actions.

These data are supported by more detailed qualitative analyses of specific cases. As Etzioni points out, there is significant evidence of Chinese aggression in the modern era through about 1990: intervention in the Korean War, its conflict with Vietnam, its support for various revolutionary movements abroad.[32] Since 1990, however, this pattern has changed significantly. The Massachusetts Institute of Technology's Taylor Fravel concludes that, between 1990 and 2008, China engaged in 23 territorial disputes, mostly frontier disputes over contested pieces of territory. Of those disputes, it settled 20 without the use of force and offered significant compromises in 17 of the 23.[33] In subsequent territorial disputes since that time, China has aggressively pushed its case and disregarded some international rulings—but has stopped short of the outright use of force. Etzioni argues that China's behavior on these issues, from island-building to cyber intrusions, can

---

[31] One argument that Chinese regional behavior has generally respected norms of non-aggression is in Ryan D. Griffiths, "States, Nations, and Territorial Stability: Why Chinese Hegemony Would Be Better for International Order," *Security Studies*, Vol. 25, No. 3, 2016, pp. 537–539.

[32] Etzioni, 2016, pp. 294–295.

[33] M. Taylor Fravel, "Regime Insecurity and International Cooperation: Explaining China's Compromises in Territorial Disputes," *International Security*, Vol. 30, No. 2, 2005; M. Taylor Fravel, *Strong Borders, Secure Nation: Cooperation and Conflicts in China's Territorial Disputes*, Princeton, N. J.: Princeton University Press, 2008.

more accurately be termed "provocations" or "coercion" rather than aggression.[34]

Indeed, a closer look at the actual events captured by the MID data shows a complex mixture of events, few of which involved outright Chinese aggression even when it is listed as a major participant.[35] Based on this data set, most of the incidents fall into one of various categories. Some involve tit-for-tat interactions with other claimants to South China Sea territorial waters, in which all parties were engaged in actions to support their claims and other parties were usually the initiators of the MIDs. A second category involved actions, such as exercises or placing forces on alert, to signal displeasure with possible Taiwanese movement toward independence. A third category included a number of border incidents between China and North Korea, Mongolia, or India. A few incidents made up a fourth category—direct U.S.-China military incidents, such as hostile intercepts of U.S. surveillance aircraft. The final category involved outright coercion or shows of force by Beijing to intimidate others, usually in the context of South China Sea disputes. These include coercive threats against Vietnam in relation to resource rights and intimidations directed at Japan over the Senkaku Islands.

This breakdown of the types of MIDs at issue sheds additional light on China's actions. In most cases, China's engagement is a product of either its ongoing dispute with Taiwan or the back-and-forth maneuvering over claims in the South and East China Seas. In neither case is China seeking to overturn the basic nonaggression norm of the order.[36] At least in this database, the number of aggressive actions initiated by other states toward China's claims significantly outnumbers

---

[34] Etzioni, 2016, pp. 300–301.

[35] These data are derived from the Correlates of War Project data set, specifically the "Narratives" reports of all events from 1993 to 2001 and 2002 to 2010 (see Correlates of War Project, "Militarized Interstate Disputes (v4.1)," webpage, undated-b).

[36] Interestingly, the Correlates of War narrative for 1993–2001 states at one point (p. 39) that in a dispute with Taiwan, "China is coded as the revisionist state because its actions are aimed at altering Taiwanese policy toward independence." If we take U.S. policy as the baseline, however—support for a One China Policy and strong discouragement of Taiwanese moves toward independence—China emerges here as the status-quo state and Taiwan as

China's own provocations. Also, none of China's actions, either self-generated or in response to others, comes close to significant military aggression.

These three issues offer a lens onto China's interaction with the emerging norms of the postwar international order. Like all aspects of its engagement with the postwar order, China's approach to the norms of human rights, nonproliferation, and nonaggression has reflected a complex tension between its determination to promote its own self-defined interests and a growing desire to cultivate a reputation as a responsible and helpful member of the multilateral order. In each case, therefore, the empirical record has elements of positive engagement alongside various aspects of foot-dragging, seeking exceptions to the rules, and outright hypocrisy. Yet the resulting pattern of behavior has indisputably come a long way from the outright revisionist opposition of the Maoist years and, in fact, is not entirely different from the United States' own approach to the order.

China's Compliance with the Order's Rule Sets

Another important means of judging China's relationship to the postwar order could be to evaluate its degree of compliance with international rules. Is China following the dictates of the institutions and processes it signs on to?

In fact, judging compliance of international rules turns out to be a complex and often unhelpful process.[37] States often sign on to conventions and agreements only when they have begun implementing the same policy requirements for other reasons, such as in human rights and environmental regulations. Thus, measuring compliance indicates very little about the actual effect or role of the international

---

the revisionist. The 1993–2001 narrative is available online (see Correlates of War Project, undated-b).

[37] Lisa Martin, "Against Compliance," American Political Science Association, annual meeting paper, 2011; Karl Raustiala and Anne-Marie Slaughter, "International Law, International Relations and Compliance," in Walter Carlsnaes, Thomas Risse, and Beth A. Simmons, eds., *Handbook of International Relations*, London: Sage Publications, 2002.

rules. On the other hand, states can sometimes slide out of compliance for momentary or urgent reasons that do not imply a general rejection of the rules.

Nonetheless, in some cases, the postwar order has generated fairly clear rule sets against which it is possible to judge compliance as at least a partial indication of a state's intention. In at least one case—human rights conventions—we know that China's compliance has been poor and arguably has been worsening in recent years, as the central government has cracked down even more belligerently on signs of dissent and channels of free expression. In another area—trade—the record is more mixed and appears to demonstrate a broad effort to comply, at least to the degree necessary to avoid penalties.

General Rule Sets

In the area of labor standards, China's participation in the ILO appears to have generated increasing compliance over time.[38] China has traditionally had significant shortcomings in labor standards, a product of its developing status, the results of major domestic reforms, and other factors, and these problems have persisted, with recent reports of poor working conditions even in the factories of major conglomerates. China's labor laws have been similar to those of more-developed countries for some time, but Chinese companies have been slow in fulfilling their ostensible legal obligations. The state-centric aspects of both companies and party-oriented unions have in some cases undermined reliable enforcement.

The issue is complicated by many factors, not least of which is the increasing role of private-sector labor standards that have taken the place of some intergovernmental processes in pushing the frontiers of labor law practice.[39] Nonetheless, the issue shows how the order's institutions and norms can provide a platform for lobbying by domestic and international nongovernmental organizations (NGOs) and

---

[38] Kent, 2002, pp. 350–351.

[39] Chris King-Chi Chang and Kalid Nadvi, "Changing Labour Regulations and Labour Standards in China: Retrospect and Challenges," *International Labour Review*, Vol. 153, No. 4, 2014.

shifting official attitudes to produce changes in behavior. Estimates of China's behavior show a pattern of improvement, and elements of the ILO rules have been integrated into Chinese domestic law. Most recently, the Chinese government, perhaps responding to a series of domestic protests and strikes and international criticism, has indicated a renewed desire to enforce the laws on the books and to "name and shame" companies that do not meet legal standards.[40] Labor law thus provides another example of the ways in which combinations of international organizations, global norms and rule sets, domestic advocacy groups, the pressure of international corporate standards, and publicity can create positive momentum for change.[41] However, China's political reluctance to allow organizing activity independent of state control continues to impose constraints on reform efforts.

In the area of international environmental law, China has displayed a strong concern for sovereignty,[42] but there is also powerful evidence of China's compliance on many fronts and with regard to a range of conventions and agreements. More broadly, China's multilateral environmental initiatives and policies have consistently reflected China's interests—but have also demonstrated a growing pattern of support for initiatives to deal with climate issues, through rhetoric, agreement to specific targets, and investments in new technologies.[43]

In general, China's pattern of compliance shows a general respect for the concept of international law and little evidence that it has undertaken an intentionally disruptive strategy of joining rule-based institutions in order to misbehave and undermine them. There is little evidence that Beijing seeks to overturn the formal organizations or laws to which the government has either acceded or contributed at some

---

[40] Mark Melnicoe, "China: New Labor Laws Seek to Pressure Chinese Employers," *Bloomberg BNA*, February 6, 2017. On the criticism, see Geoffrey Crothall, "Refusing to Honor Labor Rights Backfires on China," *New York Times*, May 12, 2016.

[41] For an example of a comprehensive survey that describes the mixed labor conditions while still recognizing areas of progress, see Cynthia Estlund, *A New Deal for China's Workers?* Cambridge, Mass.: Harvard University Press, 2017.

[42] Combes, 2011–2012, pp. 17–24.

[43] Christensen, 2016, pp. 137–150, 240–241, 282, and 319–321.

level. Indeed, Beijing has inclined toward a strict adherence to the letter of the law in certain cases.[44]

Case Study: China and the World Trade Organization

One of the most important cases in regard to China's compliance with international rule sets is its behavior within the WTO. China joined the WTO in 2001 in a bid to support its core interest of prosperity by integrating more fully with the global trading regime. Since that time, China has undertaken significant policy steps and domestic reforms to meet the conditions required by WTO membership, while also persisting with trade-restricting and anticompetitive behavior that many view as skirting the agreement's purpose and rules. The result is a complex and sometimes contradictory pattern that shows some undeniable degree of positive trajectory relative to the 1970s or 1980s but that leaves open critical questions about China's desire and willingness to honestly play by international rule sets.

Some early assessments depicted a developing country making significant and legitimate efforts to comply with the requirements of WTO membership and to enforce its rules, even if its behavior remained somewhat uneven.[45] Within the global trade regime, China has made significant concessions and undertaken policies to comply with key rules.[46] The U.S. Congress has received annual reports on China's progress in meeting WTO obligations; the 2002 report concluded that:

> Overall, during the first year of its WTO membership, China made significant progress in implementing its WTO commitments, although much is left to do. Progress was made both in making many of the required systemic changes and in implementing specific commitments. At the same time, serious con-

---

[44] Alek Chance, "How America and China have Different Visions of International Order," *The Diplomat*, July 3, 2015.

[45] Gerald Chan, "China and the WTO: The Theory and Practice of Compliance," Chatham House, Asia Programme Working Paper No. 5, June 2003; Lanteigne, 2005, Chapter 1.

[46] Combes, 2011–2012, pp. 12–17.

cerns arose in some areas, where implementation had not yet occurred or was inadequate.[47]

China complied fairly completely with rulings in the WTO dispute resolution process.

Subsequent analyses have generally tended to point to China's determination to promote its national interests within a loosely defined scope of the WTO, rather than make every effort to follow its rules.[48] Its compliance with dispute resolution orders appears to have been growing less complete and more conditional. Intellectual property (IP) protection remains an area of major concern, not only in terms of domestic Chinese enforcement but also formal state programs designed to obtain IP through surreptitious means, including cyber espionage.[49] Assessments of China's behavior over time do point to progress in implementing multiple domestic legal processes and creating institutions to enhance IP protections, including a formal official commitment to reform and more stringent enforcement by Chinese courts. However, the 2017 Office of the U.S. Trade Representative analysis of global IP trends concludes that "Serious challenges in China continue to confront U.S. intellectual property (IP) right holders with respect to adequate and effective protection of IP, as well as fair and equitable market access for U.S. persons that rely upon IP protection."[50] Protection of trade secrets remains a significant problem; multiple anecdotal reports suggest that China's progress toward better practices in this

---

[47] Office of the U.S. Trade Representative, *2002 Report to Congress on China's WTO Compliance*, Washington, D.C., December 11, 2002, p. 3. A similar early report with a similar but somewhat more critical message is Terrence P. Stewart, *China's Compliance with World Trade Organization Obligations: A Review of China's 1st Two Years of Membership*, Washington, D.C., report prepared for the U.S.-China Security and Economic Review Commission, March 19, 2004.

[48] Romi Jain, "China's Compliance with the WTO: A Critical Examination," *Indian Journal of International Affairs*, Vol. 29, No. 1–2, June–December 2016.

[49] Paul Mozur and Jane Perlez, "China Bets on Sensitive U.S. Start-Ups, Worrying the Pentagon," *New York Times*, March 22, 2017a; Paul Mozur and Jane Perlez, "China Tech Investment Flying Under the Radar, Pentagon Warns," *New York Times*, April 7, 2017b.

[50] Office of the U.S. Trade Representative, *2017 Special 301 Report*, Washington, D.C., 2017, p. 28.

area may have stalled or even fallen backward in recent years. One major commission reported in 2017 that "IP theft by thousands of Chinese actors continues to be rampant."[51]

China also compels foreign firms to transfer technology as a condition for access to its market. This practice has been common in Chinese interactions with foreign corporations and remains so today, despite U.S. and international pressure and Chinese promises of reform.[52] In August 2017, the U.S. government launched an investigation into Chinese efforts to secure technology and IP through such practices.[53]

Reflecting such evidence, the 2015 Office of the U.S. Trade Representative report to Congress struck a more somber note than the earliest such reports. It noted that China's compliance behavior is "complex" and especially colored by the use of state resources to create trade-distorting patterns of support for domestic industries. It referred to evidence that a trend toward a wider embrace of market mechanisms was somewhat reversed between 2003 and 2006, when Beijing embraced a renewed form of "state capitalism" that employed state resources, regulations, and favoritism for unfair advantage within the WTO framework, violating the spirit of world trade rules and norms. It emphasized the practice of forced technology transfer imposed upon foreign investors, a well-established Chinese tactic to wring the most possible benefits out of trade. While China remains generally committed to the formal WTO dispute resolution process, the report noted, it has also used such tools as antidumping investigations to retaliate

---

[51] Commission on the Theft of American Intellectual Property, *Update to the IP Commission Report*, Washington, D.C.: National Bureau of Asian Research, 2017.

[52] American Bar Association, "Re: Section 301 Investigation: China's Acts, Policies, and Practices Related to Technology Transfer, Intellectual Property, and Innovation," submission to the Office of the U.S. Trade Representative, September 27, 2017; Yue Wang, "China First: Foreign Tech Firms Must Be Wary Under Xi Jinping's Rule," *Forbes*, October 23, 2017; David Wolf, "Why Buy the Hardware When China Is Getting the IP for Free," *Foreign Policy*, April 24, 2015.

[53] William Mauldin, "U.S. Begins Formal Probe of China Technology Transfer," *Wall Street Journal*, August 18, 2017.

against countries taking up complaints in the WTO forum, which violates the spirit of WTO trade rules and norms.[54]

Indeed, China's behavior toward WTO rules over the past decade does not support simple "China as cheater or scofflaw" narratives about its engagement with international rule sets. China has made hundreds of specific rule and policy concessions as a part of its WTO accession process. Even the critical 2015 Office of the U.S. Trade Representative report pointed to some renewed evidence of domestic economic reforms beginning in 2013, designed in part to preserve China's competitiveness in a global trading regime and with positive spin-off effects on WTO participation. The report also pointed to a number of important trade agreements made in 2015 to address issues of U.S. concern.

One scholar, after a detailed consideration of China's WTO behavior, describes the resulting pattern as "a dynamic give and take, rather than disregard."[55] One relatively recent comprehensive assessment of China's behavior under the WTO finds an important degree of progress. "Even in difficult issue areas, such as banking or telecommunications," it concludes, "China is largely adhering to its WTO obligations," though with substantial room for improvement and progress.[56]

In sum, then, the WTO example suggests that China treats "the rules of international trade as many other large economies do: a set of norms and practices to be obeyed when fairly practicable, and overlooked when they cannot."[57] Andrew Nathan has described China's behavior under WTO rules as "emerging compliance."[58] The result is a portrait of what two authors have termed a "system-preserving power," rather than a revisionist or destructive one.[59] Yet the significance of

---

[54] Office of the U.S. Trade Representative, 2015.

[55] Timothy Webster, "Paper Compliance: How China Implements WTO Decisions," *Michigan Journal of International Law*, Vol. 35, No. 3, 2014, p. 528.

[56] Ka Zeng and Wei Liang, *China and Global Trade Governance: China's First Decade in the World Trade Organization*, London: Routledge, 2013, p. 287.

[57] Webster, 2014, pp. 574–575.

[58] Nathan, 2016, p. 178; Kent, 2002, pp. 355–357.

[59] James Scott and Rorden Wilkinson, "China as a System Preserving Power in the WTO," in Dries Lesage and Thijs Van De Graaf, eds., *Rising Powers and Multilateral Institutions*,

China's activities to gain competitive trade advantage, by skirting or sometimes flouting formal rules or informal norms of the international trade order, cannot be underestimated. State support to key industries, state-sponsored acquisition of IP (sometimes through clandestine and illegal means), and forced technology transfer policies all raise questions of whether some of the progress in accepting nondiscriminatory trade rules will be lost in coming years. China's approach to the WTO and the broader global trade regime remains a work very much in progress, with some evidence of a continuing and perhaps growing desire to pursue unilateral dominance of key industries regardless of global trade norms.

China's Role in Shared Security Issues

China's behavior toward the postwar order can also be assessed through its actions on multilateral issues outside the context of specific international institutions or treaties. How has China engaged with questions of shared concern that are under active negotiation, such as climate change, information security, and counterterrorism? In most cases, the pattern is similar: China has taken some positive steps, but—as is the case with the United States and most other major powers—its actions remain mixed and its motives somewhat conflicted, representing its complex interests.

A good example is efforts to mitigate climate change, where China has demonstrated leadership around the Paris Climate Accord and in its own pledges to cap CO_2 emissions by 2030. It has canceled dozens of coal-fired power plants and invested nearly $80 billion in renewable energy technologies.[60] It has become the world's leading user of wind and solar power. In the wake of the U.S. withdrawal from the

---

New York: Palgrave Macmillan, 2015.

[60] Elizabeth C. Economy, "Why China Is No Climate Leader," *Politico*, June 12, 2017; Christina Nunez, "China Poised for Leadership on Climate Change After U.S. Reversal," *National Geographic*, March 28, 2017; Charlie Campbell, "Why an Unlikely Hero Like China Could End Up Leading the World in the Fight Against Climate Change," *Time*, June 1, 2017.

Paris Climate Accord, China quickly signaled to other countries that it would continue meeting its commitments under the deal, a crucial form of diplomatic influence that has helped to keep others on board. The example suggests that—when Beijing sees an opportunity to gain an advantage over the United States, as well as develop a competitive industry[61]—it is capable of leading in a constructive way.

At the same time, China's actions on the climate front remain incomplete. It is building new "coal to chemical" power plants that emit significant amounts of CO_2, and it remains by far the world's biggest CO_2 polluter—with 29 percent of the global total, more than double the United States' 14 percent, and two-thirds of its energy still provided by coal. It is exporting coal-fired power plants to other countries. Powerful domestic interests in China—as in the United States—oppose efforts to move radically away from fossil fuels.[62]

Overall, China has begun to lead on the climate issue and show some degree of progress in its climate-related behavior, such as investments in new power plants. This posture is somewhat undercut by inconsistent activity on new power issues and its export business in fossil fuels. Taken together, however, China's position—especially for a country that still considers itself a developing nation—is not dissimilar to that of the United States, which has its own mixture of pro-climate and harmful behaviors.

Emerging Wild Card: The "Long Arm of China's Influence"

One category of behavior that could have significant implications for China's role in a multilateral order is its growing efforts to achieve influence and promote Chinese perspectives on issues through a range of tactics and techniques that intervene in the domestic political and social life of other countries. To the extent that this campaign acceler-

---

[61]   Roselyn Hsueh, "Why Is China Suddenly Leading the Climate Change Effort? It's a Business Decision," *Washington Post*, June 2, 2017.

[62]   Economy, 2017; Edward Wong, "Could China Take the Lead on Climate Change? That Could Be Difficult," *New York Times*, June 2, 2017.

ates and comes to reflect a broad-based assault on other societies, it will place China in a far more adversarial position relative to the existing multilateral order.

According to recent reports, these efforts include programs of direct propaganda and disinformation targeted at key states specifically in Asia, similar in character (if not yet volume) to Russian disinformation efforts. These efforts increasingly feature the same type of bot-driven computational propaganda as Russia's efforts and reportedly employ "troll farms" that pay large numbers of individuals to run fake accounts on social media platforms.[63] They include efforts to extend Chinese influence into Western universities and academia, both by restricting what is said and published about China and establishing an Orwellian system by which Chinese students abroad monitor one another for the ideological content of their comments—even in classrooms.[64] The campaigns feature direct bribery and coercion of individuals and politicians in other countries, including a recent well-publicized case in Australia.[65] The efforts include the use of economic investments to gain influence, employing donations from Confucius Institutes and other NGOs to shape public debate in target countries. Increasingly, these are emerging as integrated campaigns using multiple tools, from coercion of individuals to broad trade ties, to affect the political and social context of other countries.[66]

---

[63] For a discussion of Chinese propaganda and information efforts, see J. Michael Cole, "Taiwan Confirms China's 'Black Hand' Behind Anti-Democracy Protests," *Taiwan Democracy Bulletin*, Vol. 1, No. 10, July 18, 2017a; J. Michael Cole, "Will China's Information War Destabilize Taiwan?" *National Interest*, July 30, 2017b; Anne-Marie Brady, "China's Foreign Propaganda Machine," Wilson Center, Kissinger Institute on China and the United States, October 26, 2015; U.S. Congressional-Executive Commission on China, "The Long Arm of China: Exporting Authoritarianism with Chinese Characteristics," December 13, 2017.

[64] Elizabeth Redden, "China's 'Long Arm,'" *Inside Higher Education*, January 3, 2018; Ishaan Tharoor, "China's 'Long Arm of Influence' Stretches Ever Further," *Washington Post*, December 14, 2017.

[65] Peter Mattis, "Contrasting China's and Russia's Influence Operations," *War on the Rocks*, January 16, 2018. On the Australia case, see Tom Westbrook, "Australia, Citing Concerns about China, Cracks Down on Foreign Political Influence," Reuters, December 4, 2017.

[66] For a study of the multicomponent strategy aimed at New Zealand, see Anne-Marie Brady, "Magic Weapons: China's Political Influence Strategies Under Xi Jinping," Wilson

One difficulty in responding to such efforts is that they do not necessarily violate specific rules or norms of the established order. They may violate the national laws of specific target countries, but there is no established body of international law or a broadly accepted norm prohibiting many of these activities. The general notion of employing economic investment to gain influence, even over local political leaders, is hardly unique to China. Indeed, it can be argued that no state has employed tactics of social influence—from active information campaigns to the coercive use of trade and investment to, in some cases, covert efforts to influence local politicians—more than the United States.

Yet, as recent experiences with Australia and New Zealand suggest—and as shown by the reaction to Russia's more-intensive efforts in these areas—authoritarian states that undertake widespread campaigns of social manipulation that meddle in the political processes and social stability of other countries cannot be viewed as responsible members of a shared multilateral order. For the moment, little is clear in this regard—neither the eventual trajectory of China's influence campaigns nor the willingness or ability of the international community to generate meaningful rules or norms that constrain such activities. Therefore, China's use of such tools represents a significant wild card in terms of the stability of its future interaction with the international order.

China's Behavior Toward the Postwar International Order

In general, China's behavior so far suggests that it is determined to participate in and shape the institutions of the existing order, not to overturn or replace them.[67] However, China is not a passive "joiner" of an existing U.S. order and has often chafed against it. In fact, on

---

Center, Kissinger Institute on China and the United States, September 18, 2017; and Matt Nippert and David Fisher, "Revealed: China's Network of Influence in New Zealand," *New Zealand Herald*, January 17, 2018.

[67] Chin and Thakur, 2010, p. 127.

every major issue reviewed herein, China's engagement with the institutions, rules, and norms of the order has been partial, incomplete, often passive, and sometimes outright cynical. Its support for elements of the international order has been largely limited to those that directly promote Chinese interests. By contrast, China has shown little interest in expending any resources to strengthen those aspects that offer no direct benefit.

However, China has to some degree been socialized into the value of a shared order and is not an out-and-out revisionist any more than it is a willing follower of U.S. leadership. For each of the major suborders mentioned in Chapter One, we used data from our research to offer qualitative answers to a number of basic questions:

- Does China have significant national interests that are supported by the institutional and normative coordination reflected by this suborder?
- Has China been broadly supportive or hostile to the institutions, rules, or procedures in this suborder?
- Does it follow enough of the rules, international law, or standards in this suborder to suggest that it takes seriously the issue of compliance?
- Relative to three or four decades ago, is the general trajectory of China's engagement with this suborder positive or negative?

Table 4.4 displays the results. We display dark green in areas where the answers to all four questions are yes; light green where three of the four answers are in the affirmative; yellow where at least two answers are either negative or neutral; and red where three or more answers are clearly negative.

As Table 4.4 suggests, there are relatively few areas where China's support for the order has been fairly unconditional. However, the table also makes clear that there are also no areas of outright hostility (red) and relatively few suborders characterized by a somewhat or mostly hostile approach (yellow). For the most part, China's behavior toward the order could be described as a sort of *conditional support and emerging socialization*—a pattern that, relative to China's posture toward

Table 4.4
China's Behavior Toward Primary Subcomponents of Postwar Order

Suborder	Evidence
Global trade	Joined WTO, concessions, and reforms connected with process; adherence to WTO dispute resolution procedures; yet multiple nontariff barriers, support for domestic industries, and engaging in IP theft suggest much progress is required *Criteria for judging behavior:* • Interests aligned with order: High given reliance on export-driven growth • General level of support: Moderate to high; supportive while trying to carve exception as developing state exempt from some rules • Takes rule sets seriously: Moderate; many policies changed and reforms undertaken, but underlying policies of state support and predatory trade behavior persist • Trajectory: Unclear given plateauing of trade liberalization and continued reliance on forced tech transfer, state support for industries to gain unfair advantage, and other practices
Global financial/ monetary	Plays constructive role in IMF; its regional parallel organizations play by the same rules; very helpful role during 2007–2008 financial crisis; has moved monetary policy in right direction under pressure *Criteria for judging behavior:* • Interests aligned with order: High in the sense of desiring a stable global monetary arrangement and supporting crisis support mechanisms • General level of support: Generally high with some exceptions (e.g., still reluctant to participate in support programs outside of the region) • Takes rule sets seriously: Moderate to high; questions about policies on renminbi but have addressed over time and participated strongly in IMF, other institutions • Trajectory: Stable

Table 4.4—Continued

Suborder	Evidence
Developmental	Significant growth in development assistance, but often tied to demands on concessions to Chinese interests and not conditional on effective rule of law; empirical evidence suggests that effect is generally neutral to positive *Criteria for judging behavior*: • Interests aligned with order: High, especially if China is able to use development policies to enhance political influence; development is less politically sensitive than liberal interventionism • General level of support: High • Takes rule sets seriously: Moderate; different view on conditionality, which is viewed by some as risk to existing development institutions • Trajectory: Stable to improving
UN Charter/ nonaggression	Strong supporter of sovereignty and principle of nonaggression; has not undertaken outright aggression of its own; gray zone campaign under way in East and South China Seas that partly contravenes this norm; tends to support answers to clear global aggression (e.g., Gulf War) *Criteria for judging behavior*: • Interests aligned with order: High with regard to principle of territorial integrity and role of sovereignty; mixed in cases where China wishes to push boundaries of rule sets to make territorial claims • General level of support: High with regard to UN Charter and aggression • Take rule sets seriously: Moderate to high; record on meaningful aggression is no worse than the United States' record • Trajectory: Stable with concern about long-term trend
Multilateral security	Support for NPT has grown over the years; strong antipiracy stance; role on climate, counterterrorism mixed but helpful in many ways *Criteria for judging behavior*: • Interests aligned with order: Moderate to high • General level of support: High in most cases, even if concept for achieving goals may differ from the United States • Takes rule sets seriously: Moderate to high; mixed record and stance on climate but generally takes rule sets seriously once in place • Trajectory: Stable to improving in such areas as Korea nonproliferation and climate

Table 4.4—Continued

Suborder	Evidence
U.S.-led alliance system	Highly skeptical of alliance system, views it as threat and avenue to "containing" China; yet, has not engaged in directed diplomatic efforts to destroy alliances and appears to appreciate restraining effect on regional states, such as Japan *Criteria for judging behavior:* • Interests aligned with order: Mixed; generally view U.S. alliances as part of containment policy but have seen some value to restraint of Japan, North Korea • General level of support: Weak • Takes rule sets seriously: N/A • Trajectory: Negative in the sense of weakening tolerance for U.S. regional military role, but no desire or intent to challenge militarily
Global liberal order	Has acceded to most human rights conventions and takes symbolic steps to indicate support, but domestic behavior is highly autocratic and arguably has become more so over the last decade; supportive of some multilateral efforts to challenge the worst large-scale human rights atrocities *Criteria for judging behavior:* • Interests aligned with order: Weak to moderate; perceive interventionist order as threat to regime • General level of support: Moderate; join conventions, have supported some international efforts to promote humanitarian and liberal values • Takes rule sets seriously: Weak, both at home and abroad • Trajectory: Negative; recent trend is toward greater authoritarianism at home and meddling in liberal societies abroad
Global business order	Participant in international business organizations, standard-setting and rule-making bodies *Criteria for judging behavior:* • Interests aligned with order: Moderate to high; strong incentive for domestic role of multinational corporations and foreign direct investment (FDI), alongside desire to impose tech transfer requirements, acquire IP • General level of support: High • Takes rule sets seriously: Moderate; generally engage with global standards apart from areas of predatory behavior • Trajectory: Unclear

the international system in 1970 or 1980, represents dramatic progress and, in some limited areas, quite striking investments in multilateral security.

"Since rejoining the international system [30] years ago," one scholar concluded after an extensive review of its posture toward international organizations, "China has undergone a process of learning and socialization through participation and its attitude and behavior has been changed and shaped to favor a status quo orientation." In order for this helpful nexus to persist, however, the order must "recognize [China's] domestic realities and national interests yet simultaneously acknowledge its rising power and status and ascribe [sic] it the appropriate measure of respect."[68] In the process, China has become a more status-quo power over time—from system-transforming to system-maintaining in its basic posture. Part of this is a particular product of China's gradual integration into global economic institutions.[69]

Alastair Iain Johnston finds that "there is considerable, if subtle, evidence of the socialization of Chinese diplomats, strategists and analysts in certain counter-realpolitik norms and practices as a result of participation in these institutions."[70] He reviewed dozens of studies on Chinese participation and behavior in many international institutions and regimes and concluded that socialization works, to a degree. Yet, he also admits that the precise mechanisms *by which* socialization works are not clear. Kent agrees and finds evidence that China's participation in the order has reshaped its conception of some interests and bolstered China's "readiness to shoulder the costs" of a multilateral order.[71]

It is important to clarify the causal relationship between a multilateral order and China's behavior that has emerged from our research. We did not find that the existence of such an order changed China's essential conception of its interests or created decisive constraints on China's behavior. Ultimately, as suggested in Chapter Two, China has

---

[68] Combes, 2011–2012, p. 32.

[69] Alastair Iain Johnston, *Social States: China in International Institutions, 1980–2000*, Princeton, N.J.: Princeton University Press, 2008, p. xiv.

[70] Johnston, 2008, p. xxii.

[71] Kent, 2002, p. 350.

a clear and consistent articulation of what it terms as its core interests, and it seeks to pursue those through multilateral and unilateral means. As with the United States and other major powers, moreover, China will act to defend its interests and pursue its goals in sometimes unilateral ways that downplay multilateral venues or even sometimes stand in tension with their rules and norms.

Nonetheless, in China's behavior we do see a number of specific mechanisms by which the existence of strong multilateral orders, at both the regional and global levels, have influenced Chinese thinking about *how* to go about pursuing its interests and objectives. These include:

1. *Opportunities for direct enhancement of China's interests.* In some cases—as with the emergence of a global trading order that offered substantial export markets for Chinese goods—the intersection between the goals and character of the order and China's own interests has been very strong. It is often said that few countries have benefited more from the opportunities offered by the postwar order than China. Recent statements by Xi have reaffirmed this basic recognition.

2. *Highlighting specific ways of satisfying China's interests.* The existence of a multilateral order will not typically alter a major power's conception of its interests—but it can affect its thinking about the best ways of pursuing them. For example, the international economic order offered China an avenue of enhancing prosperity tied to international trade liberalization and domestic reform—a process that remains highly incomplete but which, even in its imperfect form, represented a very different choice than might have been made if the global economy looked very different.

3. *Defining the criteria for status competition.* While difficult to quantify, this is one of the most important functions of any order.[72] It is a well-established theme in recent international rela-

---

[72] Michael J. Mazarr and Ashley L. Rhoades, *Testing the Value of the Postwar International Order*, Santa Monica, Calif.: RAND Corporation, RR-2226-OSD, 2018, pp. 20–22, 43.

tions literature that states seek status as an important national objective.[73] The rules and norms of an order, and the sense of the international community as expressed through its institutions, create expectations that status-seeking major powers must respect unless they are willing to court condemnation. China's behavior demonstrates a number of examples of compromise in the face of perceived status-governing rules and norms. One example is its growing flexibility on humanitarian intervention, at least until Libya in 2011.

4. *Providing ready-made mechanisms for balancing Chinese power and responding to Chinese coercion.* Regional and global institutions, rules, and norms provide an architecture for constraining China's possible aggressiveness that is stronger and more responsive than it would be in the absence of such an order. Within the region, for example, the U.S. alliance structure creates deterrent barriers to certain actions, while ASEAN has become somewhat more energetic in broadcasting a multilateral demand for rules of the road—for example, in the form of a Code of Conduct. Internationally, such forums as the Hague court can be used to generate objective rulings on international law that shape the context for Chinese policy.

Yet these effects, and China's overall posture toward the order, remain mixed, in places contradictory, and highly fluid. The future is even murkier: As Chapter Five will suggest, China's growing assertiveness calls into question how sustainable its policy toward the order will be. In particular, China is obviously determined to chip away at the U.S. leadership at the core of the order and the institutional hallmarks of that U.S. predominance, including U.S. alliance structures. As suggested in previous chapters, China considers itself in significant opposition to a regional security order that it regards as increasingly at

---

[73] Jonathan Renshon, *Fighting for Status: Hierarchy and Conflict in World Politics*, Princeton, N.J.: Princeton University Press, 2017; T. V. Paul, Deborah Welch Larson, and William C. Wohlforth, *Status in World Politics*, New York: Cambridge University Press, 2014; Deborah Welch Larson and Alexei Shevchenko, "Status Seekers: Chinese and Russian Responses to U.S. Primacy," *International Security*, Vol. 34, No. 4, Spring 2010.

odds with its own needs. The central challenge for U.S. policy, then, is to find a way forward that continues to lead even as it emphasizes the shared elements of the order.

Randall Schweller and Xiaoyu Pu have drawn an important distinction that brings together the bottom line of China's views of order and its behavior. In recent decades, China has not been an opponent of the postwar order—it is revisionist in regard to U.S. hegemony, not the concept of a rule-based order. In fact, Chinese history and strategic culture are generally sympathetic to the idea of a rule-governed system (although, especially in regional terms, alongside generally recognized Chinese preeminence). Schweller and Pu define what China has been engaged in as something that it could see as "rightful resistance" to the U.S.-led order. A state pursuing such a strategy, they argue,

> does not seek to overthrow the order but merely to gain recognition of its rights and prestige within the system and to garner a better position for itself as a power broker at various international bargaining tables. Here, the grievance is not over the essential rules of the game but over representation and the application of the rules, that is, the hypocrisy, pitfalls, injustices, and corruption behind the existing manifestation of that order.[74]

Based on our analysis, this concept captures China's broad strategy toward the postwar order, at least from its own perspective. China certainly does not view itself as revisionist against the notion of a stable multilateral system, only what it regards as the unjust elements.

Interestingly, Schweller and Pu note that such an approach can actually "deepen the legitimacy of the existing order."[75] If rightful resistance produces reforms that reduce the perceived injustices of a system, that system will become more legitimate and sustainable. This possibility offers an important opportunity for U.S. policy—to support

---

[74] Randall L. Schweller and Xiaoyu Pu, "After *Unipolarity*: China's Visions of International Order in an Era of U.S. Decline," *International Security*, Vol. 36, No. 1, Summer 2011, pp. 50–51. Their analysis of China's behavior across several elements of the order appears on pp. 52–57 in that volume.

[75] Schweller and Pu, 2011, pp. 51.

and channel China's objections, rather than obstructing them, in ways that suggest to many actors that the order is flexible and multilateral and is evolving to meet the concerns about equity and justice expressed by many states and NGOs.

Despite this record, one challenge is to distinguish instrumental gestures from more serious and lasting commitment to the order's institutions, rules, and norms.[76] Is China merely taking a position to generate influence and support, without necessarily truly committing itself to the normative understandings that underpin the order? An important clue comes from the broader trend of socialization into the order. More broadly and over the longer term, there is evidence that participation in the postwar order has had an effect on Chinese thinking and behavior. This participation has not necessarily changed China's conceptions of its ends—its interests and preferences—but it appears to have informed Chinese thinking about *means*—that is, the best ways to go about achieving those ends.

---

[76] Combes, 2011–2012, p. 7.

The Future of China's Interaction with the International Order

Building on China's interests, its basic conception of the international order, and its behavior so far toward the postwar order, this analysis then turned to a more-challenging issue: the future of China's interaction with the order. That issue raises many fundamental questions: Is it fundamentally dissatisfied and revisionist, and thus increasingly aggressive and belligerent? Or is China's emerging posture still basically status-quo, risk-averse, and largely rule-abiding when it has joined institutions that serve its interests? The resolution of these larger questions will determine the answer to the question of China's likely stance toward the order.

The discussion also raised a related theme: the distinction between empirical evidence about China's current engagement with the institutions of order and more identity- or ideology-based analysis of its likely future position. The former is fairly unambiguous: Since the 1980s, China has shifted from a largely hostile and autarkic attitude toward the international order to a widespread engagement with dozens of leading global and regional institutions. China has long stated, in official pronouncements that accompany these actions, that these actions are supportive of specific elements of the order. As noted in Chapter Four, the elements of an international order—while not independently constituting a check on China's power—can shape the context for the pursuit of its interests in important ways.

From an empirical standpoint, therefore, China is *now* deeply engaged in the order and tends to follow the rules of institutions it joins as well as any other self-interested major power does. Participation in the institutions of the order, some suggested, is in effect the lowest common denominator of measuring a rising state's engagement. China has been brought into these institutions and is working to advantage itself through their rules and structure, but not to overturn them. But even this reality cannot reassure us about China's potential trajectory because changes in the variables guiding China's perspective could alter its approach.

Two broad factors suggest a potential for change. One is that China is grappling with the consequences of its rapid ascent to become a great power, even as it faces an uncertain economic future owing to slowing growth rates and looming demographic challenges. This creates inherent flux in its global posture and makes it difficult to predict where it will end up in regard to its posture on the order.

A second source of uncertainty comes from classic international relations theory—specifically, the notion of hegemonic power theory. This theory predicts that rising powers will inevitably seek to transform existing power relations, including the structure of any forms of order in place at the time. This theory suggests that hopes for a peaceful integration of China into more elaborate forms of the order might be misplaced, and it implies that China's current practice of institutional engagement might be temporary until it has grown strong enough to reorder institutions to better accommodate its preferences. The theory is not universally accepted, however, as some theorists argue that changes in power relations do not necessarily result in substantial changes to the international order.[1]

Evidence of China's tendency to incrementally revise aspects of the order could be seen as its tendency to emphasize issues of what it deems as "justice" in the current order.[2] China's leadership clearly supports a strengthening of its role in the international order (and of most developing countries worldwide) at the expense of the United States and its developed, industrial Western allies and partners. Those in Bei-

---

[1]   G. John Ikenberry, *After Wars: Institutions, Strategic Restraint, and the Rebuilding of Order After Major Wars*, Princeton, N.J.: Princeton University Press, 2000.

[2]   Deng, 2015.

jing who favor a balance of power with the United States, specifically within Asia, are becoming a distinct minority. An apparent growing consensus in Beijing is that China should seek to weaken the United States in the region with the goal of attaining preeminence.

This chapter evaluates the question of China's future approach to the order by reviewing several factors that will bear on that issue. It examines Chinese views of major international trends and their potential implications for China's view of order, China's perception of its dependence on the order, and China's agenda for reform and transformation of the order. It looks to China's behavior toward regional institutions and norms as a possible foretaste of its strategy toward the international order as a whole. The chapter examines China's emerging view of the political competition with the United States, and it concludes with an assessment of the areas of the order that China is likely to support and challenge.

Geostrategic Trends and Changes to International Order

Chinese officials and analysts now regard the international system as having entered a prolonged period of dramatic and lasting change. The most important geostrategic trends concern the deteriorating international position of Western countries and the rise of non-Western countries. At the same time, however, China has found itself increasingly dependent on the international order, although its ability to provide leadership to supplement or offset the West's declining capacity remains limited. These trends raise questions about the long-term viability and effectiveness of China's traditional passive approach to issues of global governance.

Decline of the West
Chinese scholars and officials have anticipated the arrival of a multipolar world since the fall of the Soviet Union. While perhaps surprised at the resurgence of the United States as a unipolar hyperpower (or "global hegemon," in Chinese official media parlance) through the 1990s, many scholars regarded the 2008 global financial crisis as a crip-

pling blow from which Western countries are unlikely to fully recover. Echoing a theme widely observed in Chinese analysis in recent years, then–Vice President of the CICIR Wang Zaibang argued that the crisis reflected a "turning point." He regarded it as "unquestionable" that the "generally advantageous position of the developed countries in Europe and America will gradually and irreversibly fall."[3]

Chinese scholars in recent years acknowledge the resilience of the United States and its recovery since the crisis. However, they note that even if the United States avoids absolute decline, its share of the world's GDP will continue to shrink. Thus, they argue, the ability of the United States to manage world events will continue to weaken. Yang Jiemian, a professor at the Shanghai Institute of International Studies, observed in 2012 that the United States may have "resurgent and revival phases," but its ability to "control the world economy will decline."[4]

The significance of the fact that Western powers could lose the position of global dominance that they have enjoyed for centuries is not lost on the Chinese. At a Politburo study session on global governance in 2015, President Xi hailed the broad geostrategic trend as the "most revolutionary change in the international balance of power since modern times." He criticized the behavior of unnamed "major powers" that for centuries "fought over hegemony through wars, colonization, the division of spheres of influence, and other ways" and foresaw a more peaceful future predicated on the rise of the developing world.[5] Lin Limin, a scholar at CICIR, predicted in 2011 that Western countries would "lose the superior position that they have held for hundreds of years." He anticipated a "breakdown in the international system

3   Wang Zaibang, "Historical Change Shows That Systematic Adjustment Is Urgent; Review of and Thoughts on the 2008 International System," *Contemporary International Relations* [现代国际关系], January 20, 2009, pp. 1–6, 19.

4   Yang Jiemian, "U.S. Soft Power and the Reorganization of the International System," *Research in International Problems* [国际问题研究], March 13, 2012, pp. 51–61.

5   "At the 27th Collective Study Session of the CCP Political Bureau; Xi Jinping Stresses the Need to Push Forward the System of Global Governance," 2015.

dominated by the West" that would open opportunities for China and other developing countries to reorder a more peaceful world.[6]

However, despite the potential opportunity, authorities and officials also regard the decline in Western power as destabilizing. The 19th Party Congress report noted "surging" trends toward multipolarity but also "growing uncertainties and destabilizing factors" and "changes in the global governance system and international order," which it characterized as "speeding up."[7] Experts similarly argue that the erosion in Western power will exacerbate a growing leadership vacuum, accelerating international competition and disorder. People University's Jin Canrong anticipated that the weakening of the West would inaugurate an era of "confusion" and open a "deficit in authority." The resulting leadership vacuum would likely bring about an "increase in pressure on China to share responsibility," as well as deepen greater "strategic misgivings" and exacerbate "difficulties in the coordination of policy."[8] For some commentators, the U.S. decisions to withdraw from the Trans-Pacific Partnership and from the Paris Climate Accord underscore this trend and open up opportunities for China to exert greater leadership.[9] Similarly, resistance by Western officials in the IMF to Chinese demands for expanded voting rights—perceived by Chinese commentators as a desperate move to shore up the deteriorating privileged position of Western countries—reportedly fueled China's determination to set up the AIIB.[10]

---

[6]   Lin Limin, "China's Foreign Strategy: New Problems, New Tasks, New Ideas," *Contemporary International Relations* [现代国际关系], November 20, 2010, pp. 23–24.

[7]   "Full Text of Xi Jinping's Report to the 19th Party Congress," 2017.

[8]   Jin Canrong, "Tremendous Changes in International Politics and their Influence on China," *Contemporary International Relations* [现代国际关系], December 20, 2009, pp. 1–6.

[9]   David E. Sanger and Jane Perlez, "Trump Hands the Chinese a Gift: The Chance for Global Leadership," *New York Times*, June 1, 2017.

[10]   Jane Perlez, "China Creates a World Bank of Its Own, and the U.S. Balks," *New York Times*, December 4, 2015.

Rise of the Non-West

Officials and scholars have identified the concomitant rise of developing countries as tremendously significant for the evolution of the international order. In the same Politburo study session cited earlier, Xi Jinping noted that a "large number of developing countries are rapidly developing and their international influence is continually getting stronger."[11] Similarly, then–Foreign Minister Yang Jiechi stated in 2011 that the "rise of newly emerging market economies will reshape the world's politics." Alluding to the intersection in trends between the decline of the West and rise of the non-West, Yang anticipated a "significant and far reaching impact on the balance of world powers and the international system and order."[12] Yet, despite their potential, Chinese analysts acknowledge that these countries remain considerably weaker than Western countries. Yang Jiemian pointed out that the strength of nonpowers remains "mainly economic" and generally of a "low-end of economic capability." Moreover, the developing world's "overall awareness and cohesion" remain "in the initial phase." He noted a lack of unity in thought, ideals, organizations, and institutions.[13]

Both Western and Chinese scholars have argued that a weakening power of Western countries, manifested in their declining share of global GDP, will continue to erode the influence of liberal values underpinning the formal aspects of the international order.[14] Indeed, Western scholars have noted a steady deterioration in democratic practices worldwide within the past few years.[15]

The breakdown in the informal aspects of the international system has coincided with a declining effectiveness of many international insti-

---

[11] "At the 27th Collective Study Session of the CCP Political Bureau; Xi Jinping Stresses the Need to Push Forward the System of Global Governance," 2015.

[12] Yang Jiechi, "China's Interaction with the World in the New Era," *Research in International Problems* [国际问题研究], September 13, 2011, pp. 1–6.

[13] Jiemian, 2012.

[14] Michael Cox, "Power Shifts, Economic Change, and the Decline of the West?" webpage, United Kingdom Foreign and Commonwealth Office, November 28, 2012.

[15] Joshua Kurlantzick, *Democracy in Retreat: The Revolt of the Middle Class and Worldwide Decline in Representative Government*, New Haven, Conn.: Yale University Press, 2013.

tutions. Western observers have lamented the paralysis and inaction plaguing organizations, such as the UN.[16] Chinese observers have similarly noted the decreasing effectiveness of established institutions and organizations in the face of chronic political and economic problems, such as decelerating global economic growth, climate change, refugee crises, and terrorism. Because of disagreement over values, ideals, and norms, countries struggle to build consensus for action, resulting in gridlock and inaction on important transnational issues. In 2011, Tsinghua University released the results of a major study that analyzed the consequences of long-term trends in the international system. The report noted a "relative decline in the ability of the United States to lead the world" but observed that the "remaining powers remain incapable of making up for the deficiencies in U.S. leadership." The report also did not assess a "collective leadership" by non-U.S. countries as plausible. It concluded grimly that existing international mechanisms and institutions would become less effective accordingly.[17]

Growing Chinese Dependence on International Order

The deterioration of the international order is occurring at a moment when China's need for international stability, security, and order is increasing.[18] As the second-largest economy in the world, China's interests now span the world, opening a broad array of vulnerabilities. Western scholars have noted the country's strong support for an international trade regime upon which it depends so heavily for the economic growth that has powered its phenomenal rise.[19] However, Chi-

---

[16] Vivian Schmidt, *The Eurozone's Crisis of Democratic Legitimacy*, Luxembourg: European Commission, European Economy Discussion Paper No. 15, 2015.

[17] Yang Shilong, "The Tsinghua University Report on Global Security Forum Stresses Need to Build a Sustained, Stable International System," *Outlook* [了望], December 5, 2011, No. 49, pp. 58–59.

[18] Deng, 2015.

[19] Charles Grant, *Russia, China and Global Governance*, Centre for European Reform, 2012.

nese integration into the global economy has also exposed its economy to disruption and its citizens to more dangers from afar. The country surpassed the United States to become the largest importer of oil in 2014.[20] Its trade dependence surged to nearly 60 percent of GDP in 2006 before receding slightly.[21] China reportedly has more than 5.5 million citizens working abroad and nearly 60 million travelers annually. While abroad, some individuals encounter crime, terrorism, and other dangers, driving Chinese authorities to step up diplomatic services and, in some cases, evacuations. In 2011, China moved 48,000 of its citizens from Egypt, Libya, and Japan.[22] The People's Liberation Army's (PLA's) growing focus on expeditionary activities to protect these interests reflects Beijing's concern about threats to its economic and other interests around the world.[23]

Despite China's growing dependence on the international system, the country remains poorly positioned to provide the international leadership that could meet its own demands and offset the diminishing capacity of the West. Diplomatically, China lacks the network of allies, partners, and supporters that could support the exercise of international leadership currently enjoyed by the United States. Chinese values and ideals have generally found a lukewarm reception at best. Western observers have generally concluded that Chinese efforts to promote "soft power" continue to lag.[24] Militarily, the inexperienced and corruption-riddled PLA has demonstrated only the most nascent capability to project power.[25] These realities constrain China's options.

---

[20]   U.S. Energy Information Administration, "China," webpage, last updated May 14, 2015.

[21]   Li Cui, "China's Growing Trade Dependence," *Finance and Development*, International Monetary Fund, September 2007.

[22]   Mathieu Duchâtel and Bates Gill, "Overseas Citizen Protection: A Growing Challenge for China," *SIPRI Newsletter*, February 2012.

[23]   Kristen Gunness, *PLA Expeditionary Capabilities and Implications for United States Asia Policy*, Santa Monica, Calif.: RAND Corporation, CT-452, 2016.

[24]   Joseph Nye, "The Limits of Chinese Soft Power," Project Syndicate, July 2015; David Shambaugh, "China's Campaign to Enhance Soft Power," *Foreign Affairs*, June 6, 2015.

[25]   Oriana Skylar Mastro, "A Global People's Liberation Army: Possibilities, Challenges, and Opportunities," *Asia Policy*, July 2016, pp. 131–155.

Regardless of how leaders may feel about the situation, China simply lacks the means to serve as a global leader.

The strategic conundrum faced by Chinese decisionmakers could be framed thusly: In light of long-term trends that point to the decline of the West and the rise of the non-West, as well as China's growing dependence on what appears to be an increasingly unstable and decreasingly effective order, how can a China of limited capability today contribute to the strengthening and construction of an international order that can facilitate the country's revitalization as a great power?

Questions of this type appear very much to be on the minds of Chinese leaders. In 2013, the Party Committee of the Ministry of Foreign Affairs acknowledged that while the "balance of international forces is developing in a way that favors world peace" and "China's power and international influence are constantly growing stronger," the "challenges and risks facing China's development have clearly increased."[26] The following year, China held a central work conference on foreign relations, at which leaders discussed ways to consolidate the country's international leadership role and its relations with the developing world in particular.[27] In 2015, the Politburo held its first collective study session on the issue of global governance.[28]

How China Seeks to Reform the International Order

The framing of the strategic challenge as outlined above explains why the question of whether to "uphold" or "overthrow" the international order misstates the problem as viewed by Chinese authorities. The international order is decaying and becoming less effective over time, regardless of Beijing's intentions. Moreover, the informal

---

[26] Party Committee Central Group of the Ministry of Foreign Affairs, "The New Realm of Diplomatic Theory of Socialism with Chinese Characteristics," *Seeking Truth* [求是], February 16, 2013, p. 4.

[27] Chinese Foreign Ministry, "The Central Conference on Work Related to Foreign Affairs Was Held in Beijing," webpage, Ministry of Foreign Relations, November 29, 2014b.

[28] "At the 27th Collective Study Session of the CCP Political Bureau; Xi Jinping Stresses the Need to Push Forward the System of Global Governance," 2015.

aspects upheld principally by Western countries are weakening more rapidly than the formal aspects that enjoy some measure of support by a broader range of countries. To resolve the conundrum, Beijing is looking to modify its approach to global governance in a manner that best serves the country's needs while recognizing its limitations. Put another way, Chinese leaders are grappling with the challenge of incrementally increasing the country's international influence in a manner that supports its revitalization as a great power.

A review of official documents and scholarly writings by experts affiliated with Central Committee organizations provides insight into how authorities plan to carry out this task. Some have become policies, but others remain ideas that are likely still in debate. These policies and concepts may be grouped according to the near-, medium-, and long-term periods required to take effect. In general, near-term policies seek to advance Chinese interests within existing institutions and organizations. As China's strength improves, it can be expected to push harder to revise those elements that it regards as incongruous with its own needs. Today, China remains constrained by its own relative weakness, as well as by the considerable advantages still possessed by Western powers who continue to defend institutions and norms that better accord with their own interests.

However, as the balance of power is expected to shift over time and the effects of investments in soft and hard power bear fruit, Chinese officials and thinkers anticipate opportunities to change or supplement existing institutions and organizations with Chinese-led alternatives. Long-term ambitions remain less clear. At the very least, however, Chinese thinkers are debating whether Beijing should seek to establish an alternative system or continue to reform the existing order.

Near Term
Over the next five years, Chinese leaders have directed efforts to incrementally reform processes and rules within existing international institutions to more fairly represent the growing strength of developing powers. President Xi explained that "strengthening global governance" and "pushing forward reform of the system of global governance" required China to promote "reform of the unjust and unreasonable

arrangements in the system of global governance." Working within existing organizations and institutions, he called for "increasing the representation and voice of emerging market economies and developing countries" and "pushing forward equal rights, opportunities, and rules for all countries."[29] In 2011, Jiechi similarly called for a greater focus on agenda-setting, promotion of global cooperation, and improvements to the responsiveness and fairness of existing organizations. In particular, he advocated for (1) the promotion of international development on the agendas of international organizations, (2) the reform of the mechanisms to manage the global economy, and (3) the expansion of multilateral efforts to cooperate on global challenges.[30] Official media echo these recommendations. A *People's Daily* commentary advocated mobilizing NGOs, dispatching more personnel to serve in international agencies and organizations, and placing Chinese officials in senior management positions in those organizations.[31]

Medium Term

China has already initiated a number of policies that could result in substantial changes to the international order over the next ten years. At least four types of measures may be discerned: First, China is promoting a set of values, principles, and norms that it regards as better suited to the needs of an international order featuring greater parity in power between the West and non-West. Officials and scholars recommend a passive, nonconfrontational advocacy of values, norms, and ideals that accept a low level of international consensus over controversial issues such as human rights and democracy while constraining the power of Western powers to intervene in the internal affairs of weaker states. These norms, principles, and values are embodied in ideals such as the "Five Principles of Peaceful Coexistence" that emphasize state sovereignty, stability, and development over human rights, as well as

---

[29] "At the 27th Collective Study Session of the CCP Political Bureau; Xi Jinping Stresses the Need to Push Forward the System of Global Governance," 2015.

[30] Jiechi, 2011, pp. 1–6.

[31] Ruan Zongze, "China Should Take Part in the Rules Game," *People's Daily* [人民日报], October 15, 2012.

tolerance for all forms of government.[32] In December 2014, Xi directed officials to "have more Chinese voices in the formulation of international rules" and "inject more Chinese elements" in the order to "maintain and expand our country's developmental interests."[33] Similarly, the Party Committee of the Ministry of Foreign Affairs outlined directives in 2013 to "make steady, incremental progress in promoting and guiding the transformation of the international system" based on such principles.[34]

Second, China continues to build military and economic hard power and ideological and cultural soft power, in part to elevate its credibility as an international leader. Despite a slowing economy, the nation remains the world's second-largest economy and it possesses the world's second-largest military. China has pledged hundreds of billions of dollars for the Belt and Road Initiative and AIIB, massive initiatives designed to improve connectivity and expand markets across the Eurasian landmass and Africa. In 2012, the 17th Party Congress was the first to direct efforts to expand the country's "soft power"; in 2017, Chinese leaders at the 19th Party Congress vowed that China would "become a global leader in terms of composite national strength and international influence" by mid-century. The country has since invested considerable sums into media and other means of spreading Chinese influence.[35] Policies designed to demonstrate Beijing's willingness to shoulder international responsibilities also serve this purpose.[36] Scholars, such as Yan Xuetong and others, have advocated the idea that China should prioritize the buildup of "strategic credibility" through

---

[32]   Yu Yingli, "Redefining the China Model: Concepts Impacts," *Contemporary International Relations* [现代国际关系], June 20, 2010, pp. 25–32. The "Five Principles of Peaceful Coexistence" consist of (1) mutual respect for each state's territorial integrity and sovereignty, (2) mutual nonaggression, (3) mutual noninterference in each other's internal affairs, (4) equality and cooperation for mutual benefit, and (5) peaceful coexistence.

[33]   "Xi Jinping Speaks at the 19th Collective Study Session of the CCP Political Bureau, Stresses Need to Accelerate Free Trade Zone Strategy," *Xinhua*, December 6, 2014.

[34]   Party Committee Central Group of the Ministry of Foreign Affairs, 2013, p. 4.

[35]   Yiwei Wang, "Public Diplomacy and the Rise of Chinese Soft Power," *Annals of the American Academy of Political and Social Science*, Vol. 616, March 2008, pp. 257–273.

[36]   Global Times, "China Takes on Global Responsibility at G20," August 3, 2015.

the cultivation of international partners and exercise of international leadership.[37]

Third, China is also creating alternative organizations more amenable to the exercise of Chinese power. This trend has become especially apparent under Xi, who has overseen the establishment or expansion of the AIIB, SCO, the Conference on Interaction and Confidence Building (CICA), and the New Development Bank for BRICS. Many of these duplicate existing organizations and institutions led by the United States and its allies but are more responsive to Chinese preferences, as they are primarily organized and/or feature leadership by Chinese officials.[38]

Fourth, China is building international coalitions to support its reform of existing organizations and institutions and establishment of new ones. In particular, China has elevated in importance its relations with the developing world, especially large developing countries such as Brazil, Russia, India, Indonesia, and South Africa.[39] Indeed, China and Russia have issued their own statements on the need to reform the international order.[40]

Over the next ten years or so, Chinese analysts assess that these efforts will create a complex situation featuring the coexistence of Western- and Chinese-led institutions and organizations, resulting in a confusing mélange of differing values, norms, and ideals. Scholar Fu Mengzi anticipated the "coexistence of multi-functional and multi-segmented organizations." He recommended against efforts to integrate all institutions and mechanisms, arguing that it would be better

---

[37] Li Ying, "China's Diplomacy Matches with the Country's Status as the World's Number Two: Interview with Yan Xuetong," *International Herald Leader* [Guoji Xianqu Daobao], December 6, 2010.

[38] Sebastian Heilmann, Moritz Rudolph, Mikko Huotari, and Johannes Buckow, "China's Shadow Foreign Policy," *Mercator Institute for China Studies*, No. 18, October 2014.

[39] Timothy R. Heath, "China's Big Diplomacy Shift," *The Diplomat*, December 22, 2014b.

[40] Ministry of Foreign Affairs of the People's Republic of China, "Joint Statement of the People's Republic of China and the Russian Federation on Major International Issues," webpage, May 23, 2008.

to allow "natural evolution" to strengthen the more useful and winnow the less vital.[41]

Long Term

Beijing does not appear to have a clear sense of how the international order should look beyond ten years from now. Within intellectual circles, a lively debate has broken out over the relative merits of upholding the existing system versus the pursuit of alternatives. While some experts continue to advocate reforming the existing international order, a growing scholarly community is exploring ideas on how to organize a post–Western-led international order.

In 2005, renowned scholar Zhao Tingyang stirred considerable controversy when he published his book *The Tianxia System: A Philosophy for the World Institution.* The book contrasted an ideal of a Chinese-led world institution that provided order based on an ethical logic against what it described as a flawed and failing order based on Western concepts. The book has gained considerable attention among the Chinese intelligentsia.[42] While some scholars have embraced the idea, others have been critical. For example, Tsinghua University professor Zhang Feng criticized the lack of a "feasible pathway" to realize the ideal.[43] Chinese authorities appear to have encouraged greater discussion about such ideals at international venues. In 2011, the Confucius Institute collaborated with Stanford University to explore "classical theories and practices around the notion of *tianxia.*"[44]

Zhang's work may be the most well known, but other intellectuals are reviewing Chinese intellectual traditions for ideas to guide contemporary foreign policy. William Callahan surveyed a growing literature in which Chinese and Western intellectuals mine Chinese history and

---

[41]   Zaibang, 2009, pp. 1–6, 19.

[42]   William Callahan, "Chinese Visions of World Order: Post-Hegemonic or a New Hegemony?" *International Studies Review*, No. 10, 2008, pp. 749–761.

[43]   Zhang Feng, "The Tianxia System: World Order in a Chinese Utopia," *China Heritage Quarterly*, No. 21, March 2010.

[44]   Xie Fang, "Rethinking Tianxia," *China Heritage Quarterly*, Workshop Report, No. 26, June 2011.

philosophy for inspiration on how to formulate a distinctively Chinese approach to global governance. Callahan highlighted Yan Xuetong's book *Ancient Chinese Thought, Modern Chinese Power* (2011) and Liu Mengfu's *The China Dream* as examples of texts that are informing and shaping the conversation on China's internet and in intellectual circles about the country's geostrategic future.[45] Another study on Chinese foreign policy research by a German think tank similarly concluded that "indigenous frameworks of international relations theory are already under construction."[46]

The government's official position remains committed to reforming, but upholding, the formal aspect of the international order. The 19th Party Congress report affirmed the leadership's support for the authority of the UN, commitment to reform and opening up, and rejection of the idea that China seeks hegemony over the international order.[47] Nevertheless, Chinese academics note that officials have proven receptive to the idea that official policy should draw more from ancient traditions and philosophy. The 17th Party Congress in 2007 was the first to direct officials to step up efforts to promote Chinese ideals and visions of the international order.[48] Xi has refined this approach with his advocacy of the ideal of a "community of common destiny," which also draws from classical thought.[49]

While these policy efforts may take differing amounts of time to mature, Chinese officials are nevertheless pursuing many of them simultaneously. The net effect to a casual observer is of a China that advances both integration and reform of the international order at the same time. But efforts to work within the current order do not obscure the considerable ambivalence about the international order

[45] William Callahan, "Sino-Speak: Chinese Exceptionalism and the Politics of History," *Journal of Asian Studies*, Vol. 71, No. 1, 2012, pp. 33–55.

[46] Nele Noesselt, "Is There a 'Chinese School' of IR?" German Institute of Global and Area Studies, Working Paper No. 188, March 2012.

[47] "Full Text of Xi Jinping's Report to the 19th Party Congress," 2017.

[48] Wang, 2008.

[49] Merriden Varrall, "Chinese World Views and China's Foreign Policy," Lowy Institute, November 26, 2015.

that pervades policies with possible medium- and long-term effects. The expectations that competition will intensify between the developed and developing world and that Western countries will continue to manipulate the international order to shore up their deteriorating positions provide an added incentive for Chinese thinkers and authorities to remain open to alternative possibilities.

Restructuring the Asia-Pacific Region: A Foretaste of the Future?

Because China's strategic interests and relative power are greatest in the Asia-Pacific region, China's efforts to restructure the economic and security order have advanced much further there than elsewhere. For this reason, Chinese policies in the Asia-Pacific region may provide insights into how the country might approach reform of international political and economic institutions and organizations in other parts of the world.

As early as 2006, Chinese leaders began to outline a vision of a "harmonious Asia" to guide China's policy work toward the region.[50] This represented a subset of the vision of a "harmonious world" that Hu Jintao put forward at the UN in September 2005. Citing economic trends that promised to elevate the role of Asia in driving the global economy, academic studies in government-affiliated think tanks urged the government to prioritize efforts to reform aspects of the Asia-Pacific order. The Tsinghua report published in 2011, for example, urged China to "make the Asia-Pacific region a priority" in its foreign policy.[51] At the 18th Party Congress in November 2012, senior leaders appeared to agree with this position. Congress outlined directives to "consolidate friendly relations" and "deepen cooperation for mutual benefit."[52] By September 2013, Foreign Minister Wang Yi had declared that foreign

---

[50] "Hu Jintao Calls for Harmonious Asia," *Xinhua*, June 17, 2006.

[51] Shilong, 2011.

[52] "Full Text of Hu Jintao's Report at 18th Party Congress," *Xinhua*, November 2012.

policy to the periphery had become a "priority direction."[53] Xi held a first-ever "central work forum" on "diplomacy to China's periphery" in late 2013, at which he outlined changes to foreign policy to "serve and support" China's revitalization as a great power. At that event, Xi hinted at policy benchmarks for the medium (2020) and long terms (2049), although Xinhua reporting stated that the event prioritized policy work for the next five to ten years. The 19th Party Congress affirmed these directives. The following section summarizes directives and policies announced by Chinese authorities regarding the regional order based on anticipated near-, medium-, and long-term effects.

China has exercised its influence within existing formal regional institutions but has also been willing to work around them. China continues to participate in existing economic and political organizations in the region, including the East Asia Summit, APEC, and the ASEAN Regional Forum. It is using its leadership to set an agenda that favors Chinese interests in such organizations as the CICA, APEC, and others. For example, in 2013, Chinese participation in ASEAN-related negotiations successfully derailed efforts by ASEAN to criticize Beijing's policies in the South China Sea.[54] China is also reshaping the geostrategic landscape by consolidating control over many disputed areas. Upon taking power, Xi directed a less compromising stance on the country's core interests, stating that China will "never sacrifice our core interests" even as the country adheres to a path of "peaceful development."[55] Accordingly, China has carried out coercive steps to punish countries that impinge on China's core interests in a manner that avoids war. For example, Chinese officials praised the handling of Scarborough Reef and the Senkaku Islands, in which China retali-

---

[53] Wang Yi, "Steadfastly Maintain the Righteousness Profit Concept," *People's Daily*, September 10, 2013.

[54] Elliott Brennan, "South China Sea: Beijing Outmaneuvers ASEAN, Again," Lowy Institute, August 6, 2015.

[55] "Xi Vows No Compromise on Core Interests," *Xinhua*, March 11, 2014.

ated against perceived provocations with measures that incrementally changed the status quo in China's favor.[56]

China is also pursuing policies that might result in more dramatic changes to the structure of the regional order over the long term. In these policies, Beijing's ambivalence about the existing order and willingness to create organizations and institutions better suited to its needs is particularly striking. Four lines of effort follow policy at the global level, albeit at a considerably more advanced stage of implementation: First, China is promoting an alternative set of values, ideals, and norms to underpin the country's leadership of the region. At the 2013 Diplomacy Work Forum, Xi called on officials to promote a "righteousness and profit" concept designed to increase China's appeal as a regional leader. In terms of "righteousness," this concept promotes political and moral ideals, such as "friendship," "justice," and compassionate assistance to developing countries. In terms of "profit," it directs policies that provide material benefit to countries under the values of "inclusiveness," "common development," and "regional cooperation." In general, these policies downplay human rights and the value of liberal democracy in favor of tolerance for greater pluralism in political systems and values. They also downplay alliance obligations in favor of diplomatic relations characterized by deference to China on sensitive issues in return for greater profitable trade and investment relations. Xi directed officials to put the ideals into practice to make them "common ideals" and "codes of conduct" for the region to "follow and abide by."[57]

Second, China is pursuing economic and military power that will make the country a more plausible candidate for regional leadership. The investments in military counterintervention capabilities are well known and have already contributed to a weakening of U.S. military supremacy in the region.[58] The more effectively China develops capa-

---

[56]   Qu Xing, "The Top Level Design and Bottom Line Thinking of Chinese Diplomacy," *International Herald Leader*, September 16, 2013.

[57]   "Xi Jinping Delivers Important Speech at Peripheral Diplomatic Work Forum," *Xinhua*, October 25, 2013.

[58]   See, for example, Eric Heginbotham, Michael Nixon, Forrest E. Morgan, Jacob Heim, Jeff Hagen, Sheng Tao Li, Jeffrey Engstrom, Martin C. Libicki, Paul DeLuca, David A.

bilities that raise the risk and cost to U.S. intervention in any contingency along China's periphery, the more likely countries in the region may begin to reasonably doubt U.S. willingness to risk conflict with China. Should those doubts grow, countries in Asia may choose to avoid antagonism with China by downplaying ties with a United States that they regard as of doubtful reliability.[59]

Third, while participating in existing regional institutions and organizations, China is establishing alternatives better suited to its needs. Since taking office, Xi has promoted the AIIB as a Chinese-led alternative to the Asia Development Bank led by Japan and the United States. He has promoted the Belt and Road Initiative as a way for Chinese-led investments to build the economic infrastructure to support greater trade volumes. In 2017, China issued its first white paper on security for the Asia-Pacific region. The paper proposed a vision of security, approach to international law, and multilateral mechanisms for security cooperation premised on a leading role for China and a reduced role for U.S.-led alliances.[60]

Fourth, China is looking to build coalitions to support its leadership in Asia. In particular, China has cultivated a strategic partnership with Russia and central Asian countries in the SCO. Its cultivation of ties with Cambodia has proven beneficial to Beijing in its dealings with ASEAN.[61]

The actions in the medium term suggest that Beijing intends to establish a regional order centered on Chinese primacy. In Xi's words, "It is for the people of Asia to uphold the security of Asia."[62] Leaders

---

Shlapak, David R. Frelinger, Burgess Laird, Kyle Brady, and Lyle J. Morris, *The U.S.-China Military Scorecard: Forces, Geography, and the Evolving Balance of Power, 1996–2017*, Santa Monica, Calif.: RAND Corporation, RR-392-AF, 2015.

[59] Timothy R. Heath and Andrew S. Erickson, "Is China Pursuing Counter Intervention?" *Washington Quarterly*, October 30, 2015.

[60] Timothy R. Heath, "China Intensifies Effort to Establish Leading Role in Asia, Dislodge U.S.," *China Brief*, Vol. 17, No. 2, February 6, 2017.

[61] Ernest Bower, "China Reveals Its Hand on ASEAN in Phnomn Penh," Washington, D.C.: Center for Strategic and International Studies, July 20, 2012.

[62] "Remarks at the Fourth Summit of the Conference on Interaction and Confidence Building Measures (CICA)," *Xinhua*, May 21, 2014.

have provided more detail about their vision for the Asia-Pacific region than for other parts of the world, although the particulars remain vague. For example, China has promoted such policy concepts as the "harmonious Asia," "community of common destiny," and "new Asia security concept" to guide the integration of the region.[63] These ideals envision an Asia-Pacific region in which relations are nominally egalitarian but mediated through highly moralistic politics centered on deference to Chinese policy preferences, countries resolve disputes peacefully and address shared threats collaboratively, and policy prioritizes economic development and stability over issues of democracy and human rights.

The similarity in Chinese strategies at the regional and global levels suggests that its regional efforts might serve as a precursor to its approach elsewhere. In fact, officials already invoke many of the ethical ideals and political values used in discussions about Asia's future to discuss other parts of the world. For example, China has promoted the ideals of a "Chinese dream" and "community of common destiny" in both regional venues and in discussions with developing countries around the world.[64] Similarly, China has promoted the reform of institutions and norms based on the "Five Principles of Peaceful Coexistence" at both the regional and global levels.[65] Western scholars have also detected growing efforts by Chinese officials to promote narratives to support Chinese leadership. One study reviewed Chinese media and policy in Africa, which noted a vigorous promotion of China as an alternative to Western leadership. The study concluded that Beijing may be using Africa as a "testing ground" for expanding discourse on Chinese views of the international order.[66]

---

[63] Chinese Foreign Ministry, "Xi Jinping: Let the Community of Common Destiny Take Deep Root in Neighboring Countries," October 25, 2013.

[64] "China, Africa Have Always Been Community of Common Destiny: Xi," *Xinhua*, December 4, 2015.

[65] Chinese Foreign Ministry, "Xi's Speech at 'Five Principles of Peaceful Coexistence' Anniversary," July 7, 2014a.

[66] Xiaoling Zhang, "How Ready Is China for a China-Style World Order? China's State Media Discourse Under Construction," *African Journalism Studies*, Vol. 34, No. 3, 2013, pp. 79–101.

The Intensifying Competition for Political Influence

China has anticipated the declining viability of its largely passive approach to the international order by pursuing measures with near-, medium-, and potentially long-term effects aimed at strengthening and reconstructing an international order better suited to the country's needs as a great power. However, unusual features of the unipolar configuration led by the United States pose significant challenges to the efforts of Chinese leaders to carry out these policies. Because the international system is so closely identified with the values, norms, and ideals associated with the United States, any attempt to advance an alternative set inherently risks appearing as a threat to the international order.

Thus, Chinese decisionmakers find themselves in a difficult position. Beijing advocates political values, norms, and ideals to strengthen its claims to leadership and align institutions favorably. Stronger international leadership will allow China to build coalitions to support Beijing's policy preferences, protect its interests, and balance against the power of its chief competitor, the United States. Failure to do so will leave China perpetually weak and increasingly vulnerable. Efforts to advance the country's international leadership open Beijing to charges of aggressive, revisionist behavior. Sensing that deference to U.S. demands would leave China intolerably vulnerable, officials have opted to press ahead with efforts to strengthen the nation's international leadership even at the cost of exacerbating tensions with the United States.

Beijing has tried different ways to manage the bilateral strains that unavoidably arise from the pursuit of greater international influence and leadership. In 2012, Xi proposed a "new type of great power relationship" premised on U.S. acquiescence to Chinese demands over an array of issues.[67] When this effort faltered, Chinese media stepped up efforts to delegitimize U.S. international leadership while affirming the country's support for the establishment of a more "just" international order. An article in *Global Times*, a newspaper owned by *People's*

---

[67] Michael Chase, "China's Search for a New Type of Great Power Relationship," *China Brief*, September 7, 2012.

Daily, explained, "China does not agree with the United States' hegemonic status in the world order." It argued that China "works actively and pragmatically" to "build an inclusive, new world order." It affirmed that the provision of public goods is "not intended to reinforce Western domination and U.S. hegemony; instead, it is intended for a just and multilateral new world and a genuine, inclusive, and consultative global governance."[68]

The effort to weaken the appeal of U.S. leadership as part of a broader effort to expand the appeal of Chinese leadership, while understandable from Beijing's perspective, has intensified rivalry for status and influence at the regional and global levels. Chinese officials have stepped up criticism of aspects of U.S. international leadership. Xi Jinping is the first leader since Mao Zedong to publicly denounce U.S. alliances in Asia.[69] Chinese media have voiced even harsher criticism. In recent years, official and semiofficial media have published a steady stream of commentary that disparages U.S. international leadership. A typical Xinhua commentary called for a "de-Americanized world," claiming that Washington had "abused its superpower status and introduced even more chaos into the world by shifting financial risks overseas, instigating regional tensions amid territorial disputes, and fighting unwarranted wars under the cover of outright lies."[70] Hinting at the intensifying competition for global influence, a Xinhua commentary titled "Who Is Challenging International Order?" accused the United States of violating the "fundamental principle regarding the international order."[71] Another article in the *Global Times*, a nationalistic newspaper owned by the *People's Daily*, hailed the "disintegration of U.S. hegemony," claiming that the "core of all contradictions" in the international system lay between "hegemony on one hand and inde-

---

[68] Pang Zhongying, "The Postwar International Order Has Changed Beyond Recognition," *Global Times* [环球时报], October 16, 2014.

[69] "Remarks at the Fourth Summit of the Conference on Interaction and Confidence Building Measures (CICA)," 2014.

[70] Liu Chang, "Commentary: U.S. Fiscal Failure Warrants a De-Americanized World," *Xinhua*, October 13, 2013.

[71] "Commentary: Who Is Challenging International Order?" *Xinhua*, February 1, 2016.

pendence and self-determination on the other."[72] U.S. authorities in turn have stepped up criticism of Chinese behavior, and some experts have even begun to advocate a revival of containmentlike policies.[73] Observers have, not surprisingly, detected deterioration in bilateral relations.[74]

Alarmed at these developments, Chinese officials and scholars have sought ways to stabilize relations. Chinese officials have affirmed their commitment to maintaining a stable and cooperative relationship, even as they acknowledge an unavoidable competitive dimension to the relationship.[75] Beijing has also signaled greater receptiveness to talks and agreements to reduce the dangers of miscalculation.[76] But Chinese scholars worry about the future of the relationship. While they reject the idea of open confrontation with the United States as unnecessarily provocative and premature, they remain unsure about the future. Niu Xinchun recommended against a premature pursuit of political and military power, urging instead that China focus on becoming an economic power and only investing in a major expansion of political and military power if the United States uses its political and military influence to threaten China's economic development.[77] In 2012, then–NDU Deputy Director Meng Xiangqing warned that China is currently in a period of "high strategic friction" with the United States and

[72] Ren Weidong, "The Crimea Crisis Speeds up Disintegration of US Hegemony," *Global Times* [环球时报], April 2, 2014.

[73] Robert Blackwill and Ashley Tellis, "A New U.S. Grand Strategy Towards China," *The National Interest*, April 13, 2015.

[74] Simon Denyer, "China's Rise and Asian Tensions Send U.S. Relations into Downward Spiral," *Washington Post*, July 7, 2014.

[75] "China, U.S. Affirm Commitment to Continue Cooperation, Manage Differences as Talks Open," *Xinhua*, June 24, 2015.

[76] Phil Stewart, "U.S., China Agree to Rules for Air-to-Air Military Encounters," Reuters, September 25, 2015.

[77] Niu Xinchun, "China's Diplomacy Requires a Strategic Transformation," *Contemporary International Relations* [现代国际关系], January 2013, pp. 1–8.

countries on the periphery. Meng assessed that the risk of conflict had significantly increased.[78]

Which Parts of the Order Is China Likely to Challenge?

Given its interests and its behavior and statements about the existing international order, as China's approach to the postwar international order unfolds over the next decade, we should be able to form an idea of what aspects of the order China is likely to challenge if it has the resources and opportunity to do so. While China's recent behavior in the South China Sea has led to concerns that it might be a spoiler— violating, challenging, and perhaps even overturning existing norms— China has more frequently been criticized as a "free rider," benefiting from the order while shirking responsibility for providing public goods and defending the order.[79] At the same time, the previous sections demonstrate that China has been an active participant in many of the international institutions it has joined. Ultimately, China's path is likely to be a combination of all three options—supportive participant, free rider, and spoiler—and its approach to specific issues may well reflect this complex character.

Based on official statements and behavior with respect to the largest international institutions, observers can expect China to continue participating in the UN and WTO and cooperating on practical issues of global concern. China could even take on additional leadership roles; it has demonstrated its willingness to increase its involvement by becoming the largest contributor of UN peacekeeping troops among the Permanent Five members of the UN Security Council and joining in antipiracy efforts in the Gulf of Aden.[80] As long as decisions about

---

[78] Huang Yingying, "孟祥青:中国周边危机管控已有大突破" ["Meng Xiangqing: China Has Had Great Breakthroughs on Regional Crisis Management"], *International Herald Leader* [国际先驱导报], November 6, 2012.

[79] Zhang, 2017.

[80] ChinaPower, "Is China Contributing to the United Nations' Mission?" Center for Strategic and International Studies, 2016.

the use of force are brought to the UN Security Council, China recognizes that it will have influence over important outcomes. In addition, China's conviction that the world is becoming more multipolar gives it even greater incentives to engage in international institutions and multilateral decisionmaking processes.

At the same time, China is likely to continue challenging norms—particularly ones whose meaning and application are less settled and more broadly contested—that affect China's core security interests. For example, China probably will continue to push back against U.S. military surveillance in China's EEZ and reject the ability of the PCA to rule on the applicability of the UN Convention of the Law of the Sea (UNCLOS) to its maritime territorial disputes.

In general, China will most likely try to defend its security interests by altering the order in several ways: increasing China's role within the order's institutions to ensure that it has a "seat at the bargaining table to influence the rules of the game,"[81] contesting U.S. military activities in the region that it perceives as constraining China's rise,[82] and reducing the liberal content of the order's norms.

Increasing China's Role and Influence Within International Institutions

China has shown signs that it might choose to create new institutions if the United States and its allies are unwilling to expand China's access to and influence over the decisionmaking process, particularly in international economic institutions. China's development of the AIIB and promotion of the Belt and Road Initiative may create rules and practices more amenable to Chinese preferences. However, the development of new institutions might not be disadvantageous to the United States. In fact, ever since former Deputy Secretary of State Robert Zoellick urged China to become a "responsible stakeholder" in 2005,[83] the United States has encouraged China to take on greater responsibil-

---

[81] Schweller and Pu, 2011, p. 54.

[82] Fingar, 2012, pp. 369–371.

[83] Robert B. Zoellick, "Whither China: From Membership to Responsibility?" remarks to the National Committee on U.S.-China Relations, New York City, September 21, 2005.

ity to provide public goods instead of merely "free riding."[84] Chinese leaders argue that the AIIB and Belt and Road Initiative are, in fact, attempts to provide such public goods.[85]

Contesting U.S. Military Presence Near China

China's official statements and behavior indicate its displeasure with U.S. military surveillance within and above its EEZ, as well as U.S. military exercises and other initiatives with regional allies. In May 2016, when two Chinese aircraft intercepted a U.S. reconnaissance aircraft in international airspace about 50 nautical miles away from Hainan Island, PRC Ministry of National Defense spokesman Yang Yujun blamed "the long-term, large-scale and frequent close-in reconnaissance activities against China by the U.S. military vessels and aircraft" for causing "security hazards and potential accidents in the air and at sea." In order to prevent dangerous encounters from happening in the future, he said, "the United States must stop its close-in reconnaissance against China."[86]

China has also protested U.S. freedom of navigation operations in the South China Sea and the agreement between Washington and Seoul to deploy Terminal High Altitude Aerial Defense (THAAD) systems in South Korea, both of which it perceives as intended to constrain China's ability to defend its national security interests and project power. In June 2016, China signed a joint statement with Russia opposing the deployment of THAAD in South Korea, arguing that it "severely infringe[d] upon the strategic security interests of countries in the region."[87]

However, it is ultimately China's behavior and not its words that will indicate the degree of China's desire to challenge the regional security order based on U.S. alliances. As Bader has written, "Overt use of

---

[84]   Zhang, 2017.

[85]   Fu Ying, 2016b.

[86]   People's Republic of China Ministry of National Defense, "Defense Ministry's Regular Press Conference on May 26," May 26, 2016.

[87]   "China, Russia Sign Joint Statement on Strengthening Global Strategic Stability," *Xinhua*, June 27, 2016.

force would be the most decisive challenge to the international system, but the more likely scenario, and the one preoccupying regional actors, is coercion that falls short of that."[88] Indeed, China's reclamation and militarization of features in the South China Sea has subtly changed the situation without provoking a strong military response.

Weakening the Order's Liberal Norms

China's statements and behavior to date suggest a number of areas where the PRC might challenge the liberal norms that Western democracies have embedded in the order. Here, we provide a quick overview of a few examples of such areas.

Condition-Free Lending Practices

Since 2000, China has increased its lending to developing countries dramatically and has published two white papers on foreign aid describing these activities. However, PRC financial assistance to foreign countries does not fit neatly into the category of overseas development aid (ODA) as defined by the Organisation of Economic Co-operation and Development (OECD). Many of the financial flows that the PRC regards as "foreign aid" include loans made in exchange for natural resources FDI by state-owned corporations seeking new markets for their products.[89] According to one study, from 2000 to 2011, China lent $73 billion to African countries, including an estimated $15 billion in ODA. In comparison, the United States government provided $81 billion in ODA during that same period.[90]

In addition to these differences in the form of financial assistance, the United States and China have different stances on whether to place governance and market reform conditions on loans to governments in developing countries. WB and IMF loans often require recipient countries to undertake public-sector governance reforms and financial sector

---

[88] Bader, 2016.

[89] Austin Strange, Bradley Parks, Michael Tierney, Andreas Fuchs, and Axel Dreher, "Tracking Under-Reported Financial Flows: China's Development Finance and the Aid-Conflict Nexus Revisited," Courant Research Centre: Poverty, Equity, and Growth, Discussion Papers No. 175, 2015, pp. 7–8.

[90] Strange et al., 2015, pp. 14–15.

reforms, including budget deficit reduction, state-owned enterprise privatization, anticorruption policies, and market liberalization. These conditions attached to loans are intended to increase the likelihood that the lenders will be repaid and decrease the chances that the country will face economic or financial crises in the long term.[91] In contrast, China often includes no such conditions on its loans, although loans may require recipient countries to use Chinese materials and services for development projects or to support China's diplomatic objectives, including the One China Policy (the idea that Taiwan and mainland China are one country).[92]

As a result, several countries plagued by corruption and opacity have accepted these "no strings attached" loans from China instead of conditional loans from the IMF and WB.[93] One study found that the WB has altered its lending practices in response to the competition it faces from China: In African countries that receive ODA or investment from China, the WB offers loans with far fewer conditions than those it offers to other countries.[94] This evidence—along with anxiety about what the AIIB's decisionmaking processes and lending practices will look like—fuels concerns that China's lending practices threaten the spread of liberal values and governance reforms.

Yet the efficacy of the conditions imposed by WB and IMF assistance programs has long been questioned, even in the United States and Europe.[95] Specifically in terms of aid conditionality, the ability

---

[91] Diego Hernandez, "Are 'New' Donors Challenging World Bank Conditionality?" *AidData*, Working Paper No. 19, January 2016, pp. 6–7.

[92] Thomas Lum, Hannah Fischer, Julissa Gomez-Granger, and Anne Leland, "China's Foreign Aid Activities in Africa, Latin America, and Southeast Asia," Washington, D.C.: Congressional Research Service, R40361, February 25, 2009.

[93] Joshua Kurlantzick, "Beijing's Safari: China's Move into Africa and Its Implications for Aid, Development, and Governance," Carnegie Endowment for International Peace, November 2006.

[94] Hernandez, 2016, p. 5.

[95] William Easterly, *The Elusive Quest for Growth*, Cambridge, Mass.: MIT Press, 2001; William Easterly, *White Man's Burden: Why the West's Efforts to Aid the Rest Have Done So Much Ill and So Little Good*, New York: Penguin Books, 2007; Nitsan Chorev and Sarah Babb, "The Crisis of Neoliberalism and the Future of International Institutions: A Com-

of WB programs to achieve the goals of such conditions is unclear—especially in meaningful, long-term ways that become truly integrated into the governance practices of the recipient state.[96] Some studies have suggested that conditionality can work in limited ways when the recipient nation is a democracy,[97] but not in other circumstances. Therefore, the norm of aid conditionality is a contested one, and it is not clear that divergent Chinese practices in this area will make a meaningful difference in long-term prospects for good governance or liberalization in developing nations.

Resistance to the Responsibility to Protect

While China's stance on the international community's responsibility to protect civilians in states carrying out genocide or other crimes against humanity shifted from initial outright rejection to endorsement at the 2005 UN World Summit, China remains critical of the U.S.-led military interventions that the norm has been used to justify. The dominant argument is that humanitarian intervention has been implemented in ways that violate the host country's right to sovereignty. For example, although China abstained from voting on UN Security Council Resolution 1973 in March 2011, signaling its tacit consent for a no-fly zone to protect citizens in Libya (largely because Arab League countries had explicitly called on the UN Security Council to do this), it also voted to refer Libya's leader, Muammar Gaddafi, to the International Criminal Court (ICC) and subsequently criticized the NATO military intervention—and U.S. airstrikes in particular—as well as U.S. endorsement of the political opposition's killing of Gaddafi as "abuses" of the UN mandate in order to achieve regime change.[98] Chi-

---

parison of the IMF and the WTO," *Theory and Society*, Vol. 38, No. 5, 2009, pp. 459–484; Kevin Danaher, ed., *50 Years Is Enough: The Case Against the World Bank*, New York: South End Press, 1999.

[96] Ben Fine, Costas Lapavitsas, and Jonathan Pincus, *Development Policy in the 21st Century: Beyond the Post-Washington Consensus*, London: Routledge, 2001.

[97] Gabriela Montinola, "When Does Aid Conditionality Work?" *Studies for Comparative International Development*, Vol. 45, No. 3, 2010, pp. 358–382.

[98] Andrew Jacobs, "China Urges Quick End to Airstrikes in Libya," *New York Times*, March 22, 2011.

na's leaders applied the lessons from Libya when faced with a similar situation in Syria: From 2011 to 2016, China vetoed five UN Security Council resolutions relating to human rights violations, sanctions, and calls for a political transition and ceasefire in Syria. For comparison, from the time that the PRC replaced the Republic of China in the UN in 1971 up to 2011, the PRC had vetoed just six UN Security Council resolutions.[99] Summing up China's attitudes toward the U.S.-led aspects of the order, China's *China Daily* newspaper argued in 2016 that the "Pax Americana" has been a "period of incessant warfare" caused by "interference in the domestic affairs of countries."[100]

Going forward, China will likely insist that humanitarian intervention be done only through the UN with the host country's assent and with explicit assurances that intervention will not produce significant change in the host country's political institutions (and certainly not in its regime type).[101]

Bringing Cyber Governance Under UN Control

As an authoritarian state that prizes centralized control over the press and other information sources, China has erected a "Great Firewall" to block its citizens' access to politically sensitive websites, particularly Western news and social media websites. China asserts a right to "cyber sovereignty" that justifies state censorship of the internet.[102] At the UN, China has led efforts to ensure that the rules for cyberspace governance are created by states, in part by lobbying to include the term "multilateral" instead of "multistakeholder" and delete the terms "freedom of expression" and "democratic" in a key 2015 document presented at the Ten-Year Review of the World Summit on the Information Society.[103]

---

[99] Security Council Report, 2016.

[100] Leng, 2016.

[101] Courtney J. Fung, "China and the Responsibility to Protect: From Opposition to Advocacy," United States Institute of Peace, *PeaceBrief*, No. 205, June 2016.

[102] Catherine Cadell, "China's Xi Urges Cooperation Among Nations in Governance of Global Internet," Reuters, November 16, 2016.

[103] Dan Levin, "At U.N., China Tries to Influence Fight Over Internet Control," *New York Times*, December 16, 2015.

These attempts were unsuccessful, but the document supports China's interests in acknowledging that governments have "a leading role" when cyber issues affect national security and in "grant[ing] authority to [UN] bodies like the International Telecommunication Union and others in which China exerts significant influence."[104]

China is not alone in expressing its frustration with U.S. promotion of "internet freedom" and government-sponsored censorship-circumvention tools—Russia, too, claims a right to control its citizens' access to the internet. Some U.S. allies and partners also disagree with the United States on the appropriate level of restrictions for internet governance. Still, China is perhaps the most vocal advocate for an alternative form of internet governance that contradicts a core liberal value of free access to information. This stance creates a position around which other states can theoretically rally, thus affecting the future of the global regime on internet freedom.

Conclusion: A Modified or Subverted Order?

Based on the analysis of the past two chapters, Table 5.1 outlines key areas of the current order and China's apparent desire for modifications. We have highlighted in yellow the areas that seem to clash most directly with U.S. interests or objectives. There are four such areas, although one reflects not so much a difference over the institutions, rules, or norms of a multilateral order as it does China's strategic intentions in Asia.

One obvious point of disagreement is over liberal interventions, especially after the Libya operation. While this would affect some U.S. desires or ambitions, however, China's goals here—greater constraint on interventions—would not appear to threaten vital U.S. interests. A second point of contention has to do with the U.S. regional security presence. This is a factor independent of the multilateral order per se, but the U.S. alliance structure is generally counted as a key institution

---

[104] Levin, 2015.

Table 5.1
China's Potential for Changing the International Order

	Current International Order	China's Preferred Order
Institutions		
Political: UN, G-7/8, EU, ASEAN	UN-centric with regional organizations of varying influence; U.S.-dominated	Similar with less U.S. predominance and growing Chinese influence over global institutions and hegemony over regional ones
Economic: WTO, IMF, BIS, World Bank, G-20, AIIB; Trans-Pacific Partnership/RCEP	Built around Western-dominated institutions that set rules; multilateral coordination (especially in crises)	Similar with growing role for Chinese-led institutions, from AIIB to RCEP; degree of eventual regional hegemony desired in these institutions is not clear and likely unresolved
Military: U.S. alliance structure; global arms control regimes (NPT)	All institutions Western-founded and dominated; alliance structure led by United States to preserve local balance of power	Significantly reduced U.S. presence in Asia and especially near China; unclear whether Beijing would prefer a complete cessation of U.S. security commitments; wants greater freedom of action even if against rules
Rule sets		
Trade	Detailed rules set in WTO and regional agreements; progressively more specific and expansive	Less effective rule sets that allow for China's preferred approach to state support of industries, nontariff barriers; degree of independence desired not yet resolved—has complied with many rules despite exceptions
International business/ economic	Standards and rules governing firm policies and behavior; multilateral but generally conform to Western standards of corporate behavior	Similar with significant exceptions and lack of enforcement that allows China to avoid enforcement of rules
Labor	Multilateral rules governed by International Labor Organization et al.	Similar with limited enforcement of rules once incorporated into domestic law
International legal standards	Multilateral courts consider and issue rulings on legal standards, but very limited enforcement	Similar with continuing ability to ignore rulings as it prefers (much like the United States)

Table 5.1—Continued

	Current International Order	China's Preferred Order
Development conditions	Reliance by IMF, WB, others on loan, aid conditionality to boost good governance in recipient nations	Somewhat less emphasis on conditionality but not a fundamental break with the nature of the global development regime; not a significant threat to the order
Norms		
Nonaggression	Territorial integrity norm built into UN, regional charters; focus on sovereignty; UN enforcement	Similar with greater constraint on U.S. ability to bend rules, space for China to flex muscles in region as needed while remaining below threshold of major aggression if possible
Human rights	Strong aspirations built into multiple conventions; mixed practice, some degree of U.S./Western-led pressure; great powers tend to skirt role of leading institutions (Rome Statute, ICC)	Significantly weakened international pressure and enforcement of norms, seen as threat to Party control; but agree with United States on limits to ICC
Nonproliferation	Global regime built on NPT with multilateral enforcement	Similar with stronger Chinese voice on means and ways of enforcement

NOTE: The areas that seem to clash most directly with U.S. interests or objectives are highlighted in yellow.

(or set of institutions), and China favors a significant reduction in their salience and power.

A third point of contention is over rules governing international trade and business practices, which could become very fundamental if China chooses to diverge starkly from the multilateral economic order. Finally, while China broadly supports and abides by international norms governing aggression, it is also beginning to claim growing regional freedom of action according to its self-conception as the predominant state in Asia. As it works to resolve territorial disputes in the region, China may bring to bear forms of coercion that, while they may not violate specific rules embodied in the order, nonetheless contravene the spirit of its nonaggression norm. To the extent that these actions are perceived as undermining that norm, and to the extent that they are directed against U.S. allies, they will affect significant U.S. interests.

CHAPTER SIX

Three Trajectories for China and the International Order

One lesson of the previous two chapters is that China's engagement with the postwar order is a complex process, with many aspects in tension and some in outright contradiction. It has incorporated a remarkable proportion of rules, norms, and regulations from international institutions and agreements. Its trajectory has been broadly positive from the standpoint of integration, especially relative to the 1970s or 1980s. In order to gain stature and influence, Beijing has sought to portray itself as a leader of the international community and a supportive manager of globalization.

At the same time, China's participation in treaties, conventions, and institutions has often been qualified and self-serving. In some areas, such as human rights, its role is quite clearly hypocritical. In others, such as trade, it has made some progress but continues to engage in dozens of forms of trade-restricting and industrial protection behaviors that flout the spirit of the WTO. Most of all, its growing power and confidence in recent years have led it to assert territorial claims and other interests in more-belligerent ways.

It is clear, then, that the future of China's attitude toward a rule-governed multilateral order is anything but fixed. The next decade could be a period of tremendous flux, seeing more evidence of responsible Chinese stewardship of a multilateral order, Chinese efforts to undermine that order in favor of its own regional hegemony, or some combination of both. Available evidence does not allow a clear forecast of which of these outcomes is more likely.

In order to assess the range of possible outcomes, therefore, we examined a number of possible future scenarios for China's interaction with the prevailing postwar international order over the next ten years. Based on the analysis of China's interests and views of the order, we have selected several possible trajectories for the medium-term future from a broader spectrum of possible outcomes. We identified three specific potential future Chinese approaches: (1) adversarial displacement, (2) multilateral power-flexing, and (3) uncoordinated shirking. For each scenario, we next lay out a series of Chinese policies that would be associated with that trajectory, including implications for U.S. policy. We conclude by highlighting the U.S. policies that offer the greatest leverage in hedging against the range of outcomes.

Several U.S. observers have concluded from China's statements and behavior that China has neither a coherent or specific view of a Chinese-led global order it would like to create nor a strategy to achieve such an alternative order.[1] Instead, China has joined the order and tried to improve its position within the order so that it can have a greater voice in shaping the rules and making decisions that affect its interests. It has sought free-riding more than active leadership—and it has used the order to serve its interests.[2]

China's interests will likely expand as it gets more of its resources from abroad, as more of its citizens live and work abroad, and as more of its companies operate and invest abroad.[3] As its global interests grow, its stance on certain issues could change. For example, it might become more willing to support military intervention in weak states.

Besides China's global interests, both domestic and international factors will influence China's attitude and behavior toward the order. Slow economic growth, domestic unrest, or other threats to CCP rule could accelerate aggressive Chinese behavior with respect to its security

---

[1]   Fingar, 2012, p. 366; Nathan, 2016, p. 189.

[2]   François Godement, "China's Promotion of a Low-Cost International Order," commentary, European Council on Foreign Relations, May 6, 2015.

[3]   Oriana Skylar Mastro, "China's Military Is About to Go Global," *The National Interest*, December 18, 2014.

interests along its periphery.[4] China's neighbors—many of whom have been alarmed at China's military activities in the East and South China Seas—could moderate or aggravate China's behavior.

How the United States responds to China's rise is particularly crucial. As a 2014 RAND report concluded, as China continues to grow economically,

> China's global role and security footprint will continue to grow. U.S. policymakers should take care not to mistake an expanded role for aggression. In particular, the accumulation of military capabilities, while necessarily creating new concerns for U.S. defense planners, does not necessarily indicate aggressive intentions. China has many local and regional security interests that do not pose threats to the United States or the existing international order.[5]

In February 2012, President Xi used the term "New Type of Great Power Relations" in speeches and conversations with U.S. President Barack Obama to describe his hopes for the U.S.-China relationship. In descriptions of the concept, PRC officials connect it to the "Thucydides Trap," another term for "power transition theory," which suggests that rising powers and declining powers almost always engage in conflict over the leadership of the international system and order. In September 2015, Xi said, "There is no such thing as the so-called Thucydides trap in the world. But should major countries time and again make the mistakes of strategic miscalculation, they might create such traps for themselves."[6] The New Type of Great Power Relations— although vague—is Xi's solution to how the United States and China might avoid creating such a trap for themselves. While the concept remains ambiguous and therefore contentious—the U.S. government does not want to endorse an idea that China might perceive as acqui-

---

[4]   Fingar, 2012, p. 367.

[5]   Terrence Kelly, James Dobbins, David A. Shlapak, David C. Gompert, Eric Heginbotham, Peter Chalk, and Lloyd Thrall, *The U.S. Army in Asia, 2030–2040*, Santa Monica, Calif.: RAND Corporation, RR-474-A, 2014, p. 135.

[6]   Xi Jinping, 2015b.

escing to Chinese territorial claims in the South China Sea or to the use of force in Taiwan—its implicit concern about whether the existing international order will be able to resolve clashing national interests and an emerging security dilemma between the United States and China is well taken.

However, the issue at stake is not just whether China and the United States can avoid conflict but also whether U.S. leadership of the international order will or can continue. Depending in part on U.S. behavior, China could have an opportunity to take on a greater leadership role in the international order with respect to issues that the United States appears to be stepping away from, including climate change mitigation, free trade, and immigration policy.[7] At the World Economic Forum in January 2016—the first time a PRC head of state attended—Xi spoke of economic globalization as an engine of growth and of "integration into the global economy" as "a historical trend."[8] "Whether you like it or not," he continued, "the global economy is a big ocean that you cannot escape from."[9] Whether China, in fact, turns out to be the champion of the global economy remains to be seen—PRC domestic laws tightening cybersecurity and foreign NGO regulation passed in 2015 and 2016 have not created the impression that China is welcoming to foreign firms, and China's role in the failure of the WTO Doha Round negotiations suggests that China is not interested in further liberalizing its economy.

Ultimately, just as the international order has affected how China behaves, China will affect how the international order looks and functions in the years to come. An order is not merely a mathematical result of the relative power possessed by its leading members. However, with a country as significant as China (and one whose values, social system, and approach to a number of major international issues differ so significantly from the current leader of the order), the growth of its power and influence cannot help but create profound challenges for the sus-

---

[7]   Yan Xuetong, "China Can Thrive in the Trump Era," *New York Times*, January 25, 2017.

[8]   World Economic Forum, "President Xi's Speech to Davos in Full," Davos, Switzerland, keynote speech at opening session of annual meeting, January 17, 2017.

[9]   World Economic Forum, 2017.

tainment of that order. Like any large and powerful country, China wants to and will use the order to pursue its interests—and in areas where its interests clash with U.S. interests, such as military issues, the two countries must find ways to work through those differences peacefully. However, not every challenge to the order is a threat to U.S. interests, and responding selectively and carefully to important and relevant challenges will likely be critical to protecting U.S. and allied interests going forward.

Broadly speaking, our research supports the proposition that China is not likely to end up in any extreme posture with regard to the institutions, norms, rules, and implicit community of the order, at least not in the next decade and probably not thereafter. Its own interests are too bound up with other actors in that order, including the United States, to support a militaristically revisionist stance; but its ambitions and self-image are too powerful to allow it to simply "join" a U.S.-dominated order. Therefore, some form of a third option is likely; a simple distinction between support and confrontation is too stark of a dichotomy, especially for a state whose foreign policy tends to be as complex, nuanced, and shrouded as China's.[10] Such a middle ground seems to be reflected in the statements of President Xi, whose vision endorses neither a simplistic joining of a U.S.-led order nor a destructive challenge to existing institutions.[11] Each of the following alternatives reflects one variant of such a third option. One result, therefore, is that even the worst-case future represents some degree of sustained rules and norms—a thinner, less liberal, and less effective multilateral system but not complete disorder.

It is important to stress, however, that our research finds that Chinese conceptions of its regional and global identity—and its specific engagement with the postwar order—are very much in flux. Events, both inside and outside China, could drive its policy in many directions, and its future strategy is probably more unclear than at any time in years. U.S. policy must take account of this fundamental uncertainty.

---

[10] Chin and Thakur, 2010; Schweller and Pu, 2011, p. 64.

[11] Lanxin Xiang, "Xi's Dream and China's Future," *Survival*, Vol. 58, No. 3, June–July 2016, pp. 57–58.

A Spectrum of Futures

In order to generate a representative set of futures that captures the most likely outcomes, we reviewed two sources of evidence. The first was the research on China's engagement with the order to date, which offers a number of possible scenarios for the future. The second was an earlier report in this project that examined four alternative options for the international order in general, some of which include specific assumed roles for China.[12]

Various existing analyses have outlined alternative futures for Chinese power. In 2011, for example, Randall Schweller and Xiaoyu Pu laid out three models for future Chinese behavior. Beijing could become an outright spoiler "with a competing view of how the world should be structured," in the process actively seeking to delegitimize existing institutions and either radically reshape them or substitute Chinese-led institutions for them. It could "emerge as a supporter of the existing system, working within the existing rules of the game and contributing its fair share to global governance"—something close to Ikenberry's classic notion of a "joiner" but presumably with more room for China to assert a need for reform. Finally, China would "continue to shirk some of its international commitments and responsibilities" as it focused on domestic development, "seeking to implement its vision of global order gradually." In sum, they contended, China could choose to be a *supporter, spoiler,* or *shirker* of the international order.[13]

From these sources, we derived a general spectrum of possible Chinese approaches to order ranging from extreme, aggressive hostility and revisionism to simple joining of the U.S.-led order. As argued earlier, we believe that present evidence does not support the most extreme interpretations of China's interaction with the international order over the next decade. Therefore, we have developed three alternative futures that exist more in the middle ground of the possible spectrum (see Table 6.1). These are inspired by Schweller and Pu's scenarios but have been slightly modified to reflect clear examples of a middle-ground

---

[12] Mazarr et al., 2017.

[13] Schweller and Pu, 2011.

Table 6.1
Alternative Chinese Strategies Toward International Order

Adversarial Displacement	Multilateral Power-Flexing	Uncoordinated Shirking
• Participation in international institutions • Strong assertion of China-centric vision of the region and eventually the world • Growing direct support for key processes and institutions (peace-keeping operations, development aid, etc.) • Determination to supplant United States as leader of key institutions • Consistent efforts to weaken and delegitimize U.S. power • Belligerent but still constrained assertion of territorial claims • Assertion of great power privilege above norms of order	• Participation in international institutions • Push to reform and change rules, but slow and gradual • Effort to demonstrate adherence to key norms and work through multilateral settings (e.g., ASEAN code of conduct) • Strong emphasis on alternative Chinese institutions • Gradual territorial assertion with long periods of calm and fence-mending	• Participation in order becomes compartmented and episodic; some Chinese involvement lags • Rhetorical commitment to order may be strong and China may project an intent to take more responsibility, but this is not matched with coherent, effective policies or action • Membership in institutions persists but only active in selected forums • No clear, coordinated strategy to order • Potential for more-belligerent attitude toward territorial claims

SOURCE: RAND analysis based on findings in previous chapters.

approach. The three alternative futures are also described in more detail in the following paragraphs. Which of these scenarios bears out in the future will depend on many variables, among the most important of which is the trajectory of U.S. and Chinese power.

The future we have termed *adversarial displacement* points to a China determined to push the United States from the predominant position at the head of the international order and achieve first regional and then, in the very long term, global predominance for itself. In this scenario, China continues to view a multilateral order as in its interests, as long as it increasingly dominates rule-setting and rule-enforcement aspects of that order. In other words, in this future, China seeks to supplant the United States as the orchestrator of a multilateral order that responds first and foremost to China's interests.

In this future, China would strongly support many aspects of the order—as the United States has done since 1945, and as China's interests would support. China would continue to play a constructive role in the global financial order (e.g., boost its foreign assistance contributions; expand its role in peacekeeping efforts; and, most of all, engage strongly with the UN system). It would remain committed to certain norms, such as nonproliferation and counterterrorism.

At the same time, in this future, China would strongly enhance its efforts to undermine U.S. power and the U.S-led components of the order. These efforts would include steps to fragment U.S. security alliances—for example, attracting South Korea into China's orbit, having the renminbi accelerate its trend toward a global reserve currency, and using financial and cyber mechanisms to destabilize the U.S. economy. Beijing would actively seek to replace U.S. influence in international processes and organizations. It would build parallel organizations, especially in the economic sphere, as it has done already, to drain the influence of the suite of post–World War II U.S.-led international organizations.

To some extent, therefore, this future would create incentives for active Chinese support of multilateral processes and institutions apart from those led by the United States. As is the case today, China's active search for global influence would establish some constraints in its ability or desire to wreck multilateralism across the board. Such an approach would push many states back into the arms of the United States, and Beijing is aware of this. In terms of China's assertion of territorial rights in the East and South China Seas, this future assumes that Beijing will become somewhat more belligerent and demanding as a product of its growing power. However, because this future presumes a China seeking multilateral leadership rather than unilateral power grabs, it continues to impose constraints on Chinese policy: If it were to engage in more violent territorial acquisition, China would alienate most states in the Asia-Pacific region and undermine its efforts to attain a leadership position. More broadly, this future envisions a China determined to press its rights as a great power, claiming exceptions and loopholes to any rule or norm it wants to bend—just as the United States has done since 1945.

The great risk of this first future is that it implies a growing period of direct confrontation between the United States and China, an outright rivalry for the predominant geopolitical spot. It also implies a China willing and able to take much more direct and hostile measures to win that competition. A major question about such a future, in fact, is whether such an open clash is compatible with the survival of any multilateral regimes at all.

The second possible future, *multilateral power-flexing*, envisions a similar Chinese effort to lead a multilateral order, with less direct confrontation to the U.S. order. China in this future is not a devoted adversary of U.S. influence, as in the first scenario: It is simply trying to use the multilateral order to promote its own unique interests and expand its own influence, using multilateral forums and processes as one tool.

In this future, therefore, China would not actively employ economic or informational means to weaken U.S. power in a belligerent manner. It would seek to work with the United States where possible on issues of mutual concern. It would not directly attack the U.S. alliance structure in Asia, instead working calmly to create the conditions under which the U.S. structure simply fades away.

In that sense, this future represents a more cautious and patient Chinese effort to achieve China's long-term objectives. In this future, China has determined that excessive belligerence leads to blowback and therefore adopts a more-gradual approach. Its ultimate interests and objectives remain the same—notably, establishing China as the preeminent power in Asia, substantially reducing U.S. influence over events in the Asia-Pacific region, and acquiring a growing global status. However, the means of seeking these goals are significantly more restrained than in the first future and do not involve an outright challenge to U.S. power.

From the standpoint of the multilateral order, three characteristics define China's basic approach in this future. First, China participates actively and, in many cases, constructively in the processes and institutions of the order, as part of its effort to establish itself as a respected regional and global leader. Second, however, China pushes more urgently for reform and evolution of those institutions to reflect a more multipolar reality—demanding, for example, more significant changes in IMF voting shares. Third, as in the first future, China accelerates support for alternative institutions, such as the AIIB, that bring Chinese leadership to key issue areas in the multilateral order. Its behavior on areas of contestation, such as human rights, would remain highly mixed, and it would push back even more vehemently than today against pressure to change its internal practices. On territorial claims issues, China would continue to embrace the strategy of the past two decades—incremental advances followed by lulls in which it mends fences and projects a peaceful image throughout the region, followed by new rounds of territorial advance.

In many ways, then, this future represents a continuation and maturation—in a relatively gradual form—of existing trends. A more powerful China would seek to gain increasing control over key levers in the multilateral order and reduce U.S. predominance, but in a way that tries to avoid direct confrontations with either the United States or other major states. It is also the future in which China sees arguably the most direct benefit to participation in a multilateral order that is both active and mostly constructive.

The default version of the third future, *uncoordinated shirking*, involves a China that has turned significantly inward and backtracked from recent signals that it would become a more active and responsible leader of the multilateral order. It could be the result of internal crises that pull much of Beijing's attention away from its international ambitions, domestic political problems, or simply a reorientation of leadership attention. Either way, in this future, China is far less interested in international dynamics, including around the multilateral order, and dominantly focused on a narrow set of domestic policy issues and a handful of immediate local national security concerns.

As a result, China's attitude in this future toward the multilateral order is uncoordinated and its participation episodic, incoherent, and often contradictory. It would be most concerned with international institutions and processes of the most direct domestic economic or political value, including trade and possibly environmental issues, but a crisis mentality could produce extraordinarily self-serving Chinese behavior in even these areas. Indeed, the China in this future is the least multilateral in attitude and the least willing or able to make compromises for the sake of cooperation. Of all the futures, moreover, this is the one that would see the angriest and most belligerent Chinese reaction to pressure on such international norms as human rights, information security, and fair trade. Its domestic situation could easily give rise to unprecedented levels of nationalist populism.

Therefore, China in this future would have little appetite or capability to lead the multilateral order. On many issues, its behavior would simply look like shirking—refusing to participate in a meaningful way. On other issues, it would take an oppositional stance. Depending on how internal dynamics play out, Chinese leadership could come to see more aggressive behavior against Taiwan or in the East or South China Seas as being in its interests, but the future does not assume such aggression. Broadly speaking, in this future, China is mostly a nonplayer in the multilateral order.

A possible alternative variant of this future would involve a China that *postures* itself as a global leader but does not follow through. China's ultimate actions would be the same as in the default version of this future—doing little of substance to lead toward the solution of multilateral problems while continuing to play more of a gadfly role and be a critic of U.S. predominance, rather than an effectual leader of institutions and processes. However, this would be combined with a continuation of the sort of rhetoric present in Xi Jinping's recent statements, such as the speech in Davos, Switzerland—a seeming commitment to play a more energetic leadership role of a globalizing world. The result would be a China doing damage to the multilateral order by not delivering on its promises. As much as this result would appear to be passive, Thomas Christensen has emphasized that "if China simply rides free on others and offers neither deliberate obstructionism nor constructive support, it might still undercut those efforts," in part by discouraging the constructive contributions of other major powers.[14]

---

[14] Christensen, 2016, pp. xx, 201.

Implications for U.S. Policy

Many factors will help to determine which of the three scenarios will play out. One dominant variable, suggested by the significant historical role of power transitions, is likely to be the trajectory of relative power between the United States and China. China's standing relative to U.S. economic and military strength will provide a critical input to its choices about how to engage with the prevailing international order.

A second and related variable is the balance of power among countries closely aligned with either China or the United States. China's perception of the regional and global alignment of allies, partners, and supportive friends is likely to influence its thinking about the types of order that might be within its grasp. A world in which U.S. alliances have fractured and the global consensus on certain norms has waned—perhaps as a result of an acceleration of the current growth in the number of illiberal regimes—would provide China with different perceived opportunities for influencing the shape of world order.

Third, Chinese and U.S. intentions and motives will play a major role in determining outcomes. China has regional ambitions that are unlikely to be realized under certain visions of order, for example, whereas the U.S. commitment to liberal values establishes constraints on the outcomes it would be willing to support.

Each of these futures has specific implications for U.S. policy and would likely call for a specific set of responses.

The *adversarial displacement* future would create an urgent challenge to U.S. power and leadership in East Asia and beyond. The United States would be forced to deal with a China that is aggressively seeking a short-term decline in U.S. power and influence, including through direct hostile measures. This future would have several specific policy implications:

- the need to invest more significantly in resiliency against Chinese asymmetric means of undermining U.S. power, including cyber, state-directed trade policies, IP theft, and information operations
- the requirement for a revised strategy for managing relations with a significantly more aggressive, anti-U.S. China—while

still avoiding war and sustaining the potential for limited coordination on issues of mutual concern, such as climate and North Korea, and taking advantage of China's determination to be seen as a leader of the multilateral order to constrain Beijing's actions where possible

- a need for renewed investments in regional alliances to prevent China's efforts from destabilizing them
- continued and rising requirements for regional military presence to deter any outright territorial aggression, while recognizing that such aggression is not China's first choice and that certain steps could create a security dilemma.

In the second future, *multilateral power-flexing*, the United States would face the most positive of the three scenarios—a China that has decided to take a long-term, patient approach to achieving its goals so as not to provoke unnecessary opposition and risk conflict. Of the three futures, this is the one in which China's engagement with the international order is most significant and genuine, and the one in which its aggressive territorial activities are most predictable and restrained. Nonetheless, China in this scenario is still determined to achieve a new relative power balance in the region; therefore, this future has specific policy implications:

- the need for a counterpart long-term strategy to manage power relationships over the extended time scale on which China would be primarily working
- strong regional diplomatic coordination to manage the reaction to China's long-term strategy
- improved responses to periodic Chinese gray zone campaigns to push its territorial claims short of major conflict
- a strategy to take advantage of the gradual character of China's strategy to resolve some of the leading territorial disputes and defuse the nature of possible future competition.

The third future, *uncoordinated shirking*, would confront the United States with the most unpredictable and, in some ways, dangerous relationship between China and the international order. A China responding to internal crises would be alternately absent from international processes and institutions—and rising up in violent opposition to their rules and demands. In the worst version of this future, China's leaders could come to see military aggression as the only antidote to their internal troubles, causing China to abandon the order's nonaggression norm in ways not seen in the era of post-Deng China. Therefore, this future carries various leading implications, including

- a strong requirement for powerful military deterrent of potential aggression to help rule out that option for Chinese leaders—without provoking further paranoia in what will be a highly unstable Chinese political context.
- the requirement for strong regional diplomatic coordination to deal with an angry and unpredictable China.
- work to generate leadership in international institutions absent a significant Chinese role—to find alternatives to Beijing's voice on such issues as climate and nonproliferation.
- efforts to generate positive benefits for China from key international institutions and processes, especially in the economic sphere.
- efforts to resolve one or more selected territorial disputes to ease the risk of future conflict.

Preparing for a Range of Possible Futures

Following a pattern established by many rising powers, China is questioning features of an international order that nurtured its rise. Beijing appears to have concluded that the realization of national revitalization will require the country to shape an international order that better accommodates its interests and idiosyncratic norms and values. As the world's second largest economy, China may chafe at aspects of U.S. leadership, but Beijing recognizes that it lacks the ability to seriously contest that leadership.

Whether China will ever reach the point at which it opts to hazard war to become the world leader is unclear. In a study of the seven power transition scenarios between global lead economies and their challengers since the 1500s, scholars David Rapkin and William Thompson identified 13 indicators that a challenger country might have sufficient inducement to risk conflict to contest leadership of the global system.[15] They concluded that the most important factors remain variable enough that, at this point, it is difficult to determine whether China will truly have sufficient inducement or ability to openly contest leadership of the global system.[16]

There are indeed many reasons to doubt China's ability to expand its international leadership role over the medium and long terms. First and foremost, the geostrategic trends that could open opportunities for greater Chinese leadership on the world stage remain far from determined. The slowing Chinese economy and uneven progress of the non-West, as well as the resurgence of the U.S. economy, could constrain China's ability to realize any hope to revamp the international order. Moreover, Beijing's efforts to cultivate political allies and advance its ideals have received a mixed reaction. Even in its own backyard, Chinese power has received at best a cool reception. In many cases, Asian countries have sought stronger ties with the United States to balance Chinese influence. It is also unclear what sort of ideals and theories for a "post-Western" international order China might embrace, if any. It is possible that future leaders could conclude that existing mechanisms work best, and that reform or slight changes might suffice for China's purposes, especially if the country's leverage turns out to be less than anticipated, perhaps owing to economic slowdown.

However, the alternative cannot be ruled out either. If China succeeds in setting economic growth on a more sustainable foundation and establishing itself as the world's leading technological innovator, its claims to international leadership will become more plausible. Tensions with the United States are already growing over China's efforts

---

[15] David Rapkin and William Thompson, *Transition Scenarios: China and the United States in the Twenty-First Century*, Chicago: University of Chicago Press, 2013, p. 84.

[16] Rapkin and Thompson, 2013, p. 211.

to increase its influence over global technical standards and market share. If the Chinese can advance norms, principles, and values that resonate with developing powers more than those of the West, and if China can seize a commanding share of global markets, Beijing may conclude that the legitimacy gained from such support should entitle it to greater international authority. Competition under these conditions could intensify even more sharply, although, even under these conditions, conflict is hardly assured.

For years, Western countries have called on China to take on greater global responsibilities. Beijing appears to be mulling over how to step up its international profile, sensing a multitude of potential strategic benefits. But as it pursues a greater degree of international leadership, it is determined to do so on its own terms, not those of the United States and its allies. How to manage the opportunity to be gained from Chinese cooperation while limiting the risks of a damaging competition for leadership will likely become an increasingly important challenge for U.S. decisionmakers.

CHAPTER SEVEN

Conclusions and Recommendations

This study has painted a complex portrait of China's attitude and behavior toward the postwar international order. China's approach to the order cannot be characterized as either hostile or supportive—it is somewhere in between. Nonetheless, the evidence does support some qualified conclusions. The basic trajectory of China's interaction with the order has been positive over the past three decades. A desire to be viewed as a responsible leader of a multilateral order—albeit one displaying increasing respect for Chinese power—has at times served to constrain Chinese actions, at least at the margins. However, China seems determined to realize certain ambitions for its own relative power that could challenge certain rules and norms of the international order.

Toward a Stable Competition in the Context of a Shared Order

This analysis of China's possible attitude toward the postwar international order reflects the most fundamental theme about the future of Sino-American relations in general: The relationship will be anything but simple—and yet it remains possible, given what we know today, for the United States to strive for a stable competition that does not descend into an openly adversarial situation and that continues to provide room for collaboration on issues of mutual concern.

As we noted at the beginning of this report, our evaluation of the evidence leads us to rule out the most extreme scenarios, at least for the time being—futures in which China either simply accedes to a U.S.-

led order and meekly follows its rules, or it becomes so aggressively revisionist that it aims to tear down most of the institutions, rules, and norms that have arisen since 1945. The most likely outcomes during the next decade are some variant of a middle ground between such extremes, outcomes that will be full of tensions and contradictions to manage. China will be neither a friend nor an enemy of the global order, and the United States—as well as many other states—will have to manage the resulting complexities.

In the process, our analysis suggests that a robust multilateral order will offer the United States and its friends and allies with tremendous advantages for complementing other instruments of national power to achieve a stable competition that allows multilateral cooperation in a number of important areas. As other reports in this study have suggested, a strong international order helps to set the rules by which states are expected to play, creates the shared understandings that states must respect in order to win recognition and status, and fosters the institutions that leaders of the order are expected to support. In short, a strong international order creates the framework within which the United States and others can hold a rising China accountable to certain behaviors. They could do so in the absence of an order, of course, but it would be a more complicated and fractious, and ultimately less effective, strategy.

At the same time, U.S. strategy and policy must encourage China to prefer moderate actions undertaken with a multilateral spirit to unilateral coercion. Part of the challenge is to "demonstrate that Chinese nationalist greatness can best be achieved in the new century through participation in global projects," Christensen has argued.[1] This will be extremely difficult at a time when China's rising power—and self-perception of growing influence—will make Beijing, in some cases, less likely to compromise.

This report has recommended a two-part U.S. approach to China and the international order. First, the United States should undertake a number of more energetic policies—and should be willing to accept some degree of geopolitical risk—in order to recruit China, even with

---

[1]   Christensen, 2016, pp. xxi.

its different attitudes toward a number of major issues, as a coleader of that order. This effort would, in effect, attempt to determine whether China is truly willing to reflect the vision represented in Xi's speech at Davos, promising to support free and open trade, nonaggression, and other key norms in a globalizing world. Our analysis does not suggest that such an effort will be successful across the board or will avoid increasing Chinese assertiveness, especially in areas where it perceives an opportunity to undermine U.S. influence and power. However, because of China's crucial role in a number of multilateral issues (from trade to climate) and because more hostile alternatives risk devastating conflict, using the established order to try to shape and channel Chinese ambitions should remain the priority U.S. approach.

However, the second approach is that clear evidence of China's regional ambitions, as well as conflicting evidence about its potential to manage those ambitions short of a much more pointed clash with the United States, demand that the United States undertake powerful strategies to hedge against the failure of the first approach. The major difficulty will be keeping the hedging actions from creating such threat perceptions in China that they undermine the dominant approach of providing China with a greater ownership stake in a multilateral order. This essential challenge—sustaining a shared order with an increasingly powerful and assertive state with different values from the United States and different opinions on a wide range of major policy issues— is arguably the central U.S. foreign policy problem for the coming decades.

Taking these broad themes into account—as well as the complexity of China's behavior to date—this study offers three leading findings about the relationship of China to the international order, summarized in the following section. This analysis also supports a number of specific policy recommendations.

Putting China's Approach to the Postwar Order into Perspective

This analysis produced three general findings that offer clues to interpreting China's interaction with the postwar international order.

First, *China should be viewed not as an opponent or saboteur of the postwar international order, but rather as a conditional supporter.* Broadly speaking, since China undertook a new policy of international engagement in the 1980s—and putting aside the areas (liberal values and human rights) where the CCP has the greatest degree of conflict with the U.S.-led order—the level and quality of its participation in the order rival those of most other states. It has come to see multilateral institutions and processes as important, if not essential, for the achievement of its interests. Like the United States and other major powers, it has demanded exceptions to rules and norms when it saw vital interests at stake, but those cases do not invalidate the impressive level of participation it has achieved.

Second, looking forward, *a strengthened and increasingly multilateral international order can provide a critical tool that the United States and other countries can use to shape and constrain rising Chinese power.* This effect can be seen in many ways: reforms China has undertaken as part of its WTO membership; increased efforts to help mediate international disputes, such as North Korea; and more. A key value of the order, we have argued in other works for this project, is to create the shared standards against which individual states' actions are judged for their legitimacy (i.e., to fashion the norms to which states must adhere for the purposes of status, prestige, and influence). Such a shared order cannot alone determine states' behavior: It must be complemented with other factors, such as U.S. leadership and military power, as well as supportive socioeconomic trends. However, a vibrant multilateral order can play a critical role in guiding and shaping the ways in which China seeks to achieve its burgeoning ambitions.

Finally, *modifications to the order on the margins in response to Chinese preferences pose less threat to a stable international system than does a future in which China is alienated from that system.* Some observers have been concerned about the implications of alternative standards or institutions promoted by China, from the use of the AIIB to create an alternative to WB investments in the region to China's refusal to attach conditions (in terms of human rights, rule of law, or labor or environmental standards) to its development projects. China's approach to nonproliferation also differs from that of the United States. The United States should continue to press for norms it believes in—but, in general, a future order with modified but still generally positive norms and strong Chinese ownership and backing would serve U.S. interests far more than a partial order, increasingly opposed by China, that embodies a more unadulterated version of those norms.

In considering China's future role in the order, the United States can take reassurance from the relative degree of legitimacy and trust engendered by the U.S. and Chinese political systems. With some significant exceptions, U.S. power—especially in Asia—has been viewed as a stabilizing and largely nonthreatening factor that has contributed to regional peace and prosperity. However, China's ability to realize this ambition is constrained by the fact that many Asian countries remain distrustful of Chinese power. To the extent that Beijing attempts to assert regional dominance through multilateral efforts that fail to adequately account for the interests of other countries, it will produce—and is already producing—countervailing reactions from regional states. Therefore, there are limits to how much China can use the Belt and Road Initiative and other economic and security-related efforts to bribe or coerce participating nations into doing its bidding. In its effort to shape an economic and security order in Asia to its advantage, China faces many hurdles.

U.S. Strategy Toward China and a Shared Order

This analysis produced a number of possible policy recommendations for the United States in regard to China and the international order. The basic goal of these steps would be to shape China's growing influence in ways that preserve the space for a meaningful set of norms, rules, and institutions to help regulate international competition.

The Foundation for a Strategy: Three Insights
In shaping such a strategy, this report suggests three broad insights that can inform the U.S. approach to China in the context of a multilateral order. First, as stressed earlier, *China's general trajectory has been positive, but its ultimate position in regard to any meaningfully shared order remains to be determined.* Its ambitions, appreciation for its own expanding power, grievance-fueled sense of entitlement, and nationalism could eventually cause it to turn away from multilateralism and adopt a more aggressive and revisionist posture. Based on China's current perception of its interests and the best ways of pursuing them, such an extreme outcome appears unlikely. However, there is no reason to assume that China will remain committed to a course of increasing integration into multilateral forms, norms, and rules.

This risk points to the importance of a strong, nuanced U.S. strategy for hedging against Chinese power. This is no reason to leap immediately to the conclusion that the only or best way of doing this is by building up military power or by taking steps—such as opposing the AIIB—to contain Chinese power. Barring an economic or social calamity in China, the growth of that power is inevitable. This study suggests that the postwar international order and its associated rules and norms offer a more promising framework by which the United States may be able to shape and channel China's growing power. The components of a multilateral order cannot serve this purpose alone; the backing of credible U.S. military power for deterrence, for example, is also an important factor. However, the United States should think first and foremost about employing one of its leading forms of competitive advantage—its role as leader and sponsor of a shared order that many states view as in their interests—to help constrain Chinese ambitions.

At the same time, our findings emphasize the constructive role that a credible U.S. regional posture can play in supporting, rather than undermining, an effort to offer China a multilateral path to the greater influence it seeks. Credible U.S. power has actually had the effect of encouraging China to engage the region in peaceful terms through multilateral institutions—believing that showing a moderate and order-promoting face was the best way to neutralize U.S. containment efforts.[2] This effect can be undermined if the United States goes too far in efforts to project military power or regional predominance. However, our research emphasizes the requirement for a nuanced, carefully integrated combination of quiet but firm diplomacy; effective but not provocative military capabilities; and engagement of the region—and China—through the lens of the rules, norms, and institutions of a shared order.

A second broad insight from this study is that *the geopolitical challenge of China and the order must be resolved gradually, piece by painstaking piece, rather than all at once.* The complex and mixed motives of China's interaction with multilateral rules and norms would tend to rule out any simple "grand bargains." This study suggests, for example, that it would be difficult to develop a fresh, wide-ranging "security architecture for East Asia" that would promulgate rules of conduct and resolve many ongoing disputes. Given China's kaleidoscope of goals, interests, and views about the multilateral order, such a comprehensive solution is likely a bridge too far. But that also implies that the lack of such a comprehensive solution should not be viewed as a failure; the standard for U.S. strategy is one of incremental progress. If each year reflects a handful of new discrete resolutions—an agreement on one piece of the IP issue, a small fishing rights accord with one or more countries, a new Chinese reaffirmation of the ASEAN Code of Conduct, steadily increasing Chinese contributions to the IMF and UN peacekeeping programs—it should be viewed as a success.

The final insight suggested by this analysis is that *China's territorial claims regarding Taiwan and the East and South China Seas reflect specific issues, rather than a generalized rebellion against the norms of the order.* China has generally supported the norm of sovereignty and its accompanying prohibition on territorial aggression. It has joined with the United States in opposing aggressive actions in other regions. Since 1979, China has not been involved in large-scale aggression of its own. It has chosen a preferred strategy of long-term political and economic integration with Taiwan (rather than military aggression) and undertaken lower-threshold gray zone activities (rather than outright military

---

2   Christensen, 2016, pp. 23, 193–195, 292.

action) in the East and South China Seas. None of this is to downplay the significance of the actions—but it is to suggest that China's efforts to expand its territorial control reflect specific claims in limited areas. These claims do not imply a generalized revisionist stance, and they do not necessarily presage aggression against other states.

The important lesson is that the United States should not allow disputes over these claims to undermine its larger effort to work with China in the context of a multilateral order. Washington can push back appropriately against coercion in those areas. However, in doing so, it should bear in mind that there are many indicators of China's engagement with a multilateral order, and disputes over its claims represents only one side.

U.S. Strategy Toward China and a Shared Order: Collaborative Initiatives

These insights, as well as the preceding analysis as a whole, point to the potential utility of a two-part U.S. approach to the future of China's engagement with the international order. First, on the positive side of the ledger, *the United States should develop a comprehensive strategy to work toward expanding China's leadership role in the international order.* This will demand compromise on some issues and a willingness to see China build institutions and processes that it will lead. This recommendation flows from a general assumption: The growth of Chinese power is inevitable and not something the United States can or should oppose per se but instead should seek to shape. In the process, the United States should use this effort at sharing the order to build strong, long-term relationships with Chinese officials at all levels and in all issue areas.

This recommendation goes beyond the component of U.S.-China strategy commonly termed "engagement" or recruiting China "into" the existing order. It will demand a U.S. willingness to accept modified rules and norms that preserve the essential spirit of the order but work to partly accommodate China's different perspectives on issues. Simply defending existing institutions, rules, and norms from any change would set up an inevitably hostile relationship and begin a process of pitting China against the United States and the international order.[3]

It is counterproductive to confront China on the assumption that its role in various areas, such as financial institutions, will be hostile and destructive.[4] The challenge is to welcome and shape China's participation, rather than to oppose it, while deciding on a few specific conditions on which the United States will not compromise. The assumption that China would simply integrate into a U.S.-led system has proven too simple—but that does not mean that the opposite assumption, that it is intent on ruining that system, is any more valid.

On the other hand, as Christensen has argued, it is equally questionable to engage China in generic efforts at "reassurance" or to sign up to joint initiatives guided by commonly agreed phrases that the two sides will interpret very differently.[5] The centerpiece of any U.S. effort to engage China through the mechanism of a shared order will have to be worked out through initiatives on specific issues with clearly identified goals—goals that can be presented to China's leaders as directly benefiting China's interests.

This first component of the strategy would have specific policy implications for issues relevant to a shared order. The broad rule would be to accept growing Chinese activism and influence on issues and in specific ways that are at least neutral toward the basic norms and principles of the order. Examples include the following:

- Offer public assurances, from the president on down, that the United States welcomes China as a sponsor of a globalizing order, but make this intention a reality through concrete, issue-specific initiatives.
- Manage the interaction, in part, through a standing, high-level mechanism, such as the U.S.-China Strategic and Economic Dialogue and similar venues employed in the past.

---

[3] Olson and Prestowitz, 2011, p. 84.

[4] McDowell, 2015.

[5] Christensen, 2016, pp. 252–253, 299.

- Broadly speaking, the United States should welcome and join new regional economic institutions sponsored by China, as long as these institutions abide by basic criteria and conditions established by their global counterparts (as the AIIB has done so far, for example, in regard to WB standards).
- Support, rather than oppose, a bigger role for China in the leadership of key UN processes, such as peacekeeping operations.
- Building on reforms already in place, support a gradually more significant role for China in the IMF, including the provision of larger voting shares.
- Welcome Chinese investment and aid in Africa and the Belt and Road Initiative's proposed partner countries, as long as these do not come with coercive political conditions—an outcome the recipient countries also would be keen to avoid.
- Work in close coordination with China on key regional issues of mutual concern, such as North Korea, taking seriously the fact that China largely shares U.S. interests and might simply have different ideas about the best way to achieve them.

The rule in these processes is that the United States can be more hesitant about growing Chinese influence in the order in places where China has proven distinctly unwilling to meet key standards or continues to fall short of key benchmarks. That would suggest a more conditional and gradual support for Chinese initiatives in a number of areas. These could include accepting the *renminbi* as a global reserve currency, something the United States should continue to make conditional on significant domestic economic reforms, as well as the overall geopolitical goals sought by the Belt and Road Initiative.

Finally, a strategy for more actively sharing the multilateral order with China—but one that recognizes the first insight noted in this section, that the resolution of problems will be gradual rather than sudden—would accelerate diplomatic efforts to make partial, even symbolic progress in at least three important areas of potential dispute related to the order. These include, first, the issue area of *trade*. The United States should press China for a series of ongoing reforms in such areas as IP protection, technology transfer demands, and cyber theft of industrial information, as well as traditional areas of nontariff protections. The problem does not have to be solved overnight, but the trajectory must be positive, especially in areas of IP theft, cyber intrusions for industrial gain, and technology transfer.

More generally, the United States should reaffirm and enforce the principle of reciprocity in international economic institutions. One area of Chinese pressure on the current order that should be of particular concern is its ongoing effort to resist true reciprocity in economic institutions. China routinely, and perhaps increasingly, uses tools (such as nontariff barriers and industrial policy) to sidestep the reciprocal liberalization intended in major trade deals. If this trend were to accelerate, it would threaten the most fundamental basis for cooperation under the order—a sense of mutual economic benefit from the order's economic institutions.

A second area demanding gradual progress in established shared standards is *information security*. China's cyber activities risk creating a generalized sense of ongoing conflict between the two countries. The United States should redouble ongoing efforts to achieve something that will surely be slow in coming—a long-term code of conduct for cyber activities. A recent RAND report offered a number of policy recommendations for achieving progress.[6]

Finally, the third area demanding progress in shared norms and standards is *disputes over Chinese territorial claims in Asia*. This area represents perhaps China's most apparent potential challenge to norms of the order, in that Chinese behavior has become belligerent and seemingly unconcerned with meeting others' interests. Indeed, a major challenge in this issue is how little overlap there is between Chinese claims and ambitions and the interests of regional states. There is a significant zero-sum aspect to these issues.

Moreover, treatments of these disputes seldom lay out specific road maps for progress. Because of the complexity of the disputes and the zero-sum character of many claims, there is no obvious set of easy compromises that could offer an initial path toward resolution. Beijing

---

[6]   Scott W. Harold, Martin C. Libicki, and Astrid Stuth Cevallos, *Getting to Yes with China in Cyberspace*, Santa Monica, Calif.: RAND Corporation, RR-1335-RC, 2016.

has seemed especially resistant to any such compromises of late, taking the implicit position that it has laid out its claims and expects one day to realize them.

The United States—working closely with regional states—can also set the context for a more peaceful and gradual resolution of dispute issues by promoting dialogue and multilateral cooperation against shared threats. The further development of codes of conduct, using the existing ASEAN framework as a basis and inspiration, could play an important role in deepening the expectations for state behavior in regard to such claims. Given the sensitivities of regional states, the United States might not be able to lead such negotiations, but it can encourage and support them.

This issue area provides an example of the leverage that a multilateral order provides to U.S. diplomacy. The essential U.S. geopolitical objective is to prevent not the growth of Chinese power or even relative regional preeminence—developments that are largely inevitable—but degrees of Chinese belligerence and coercion that undermine the potential for a stable, peaceful and prosperous region characterized by self-determination and the rule of law. All regional states share that objective with the United States, even if they do not always choose the same means to pursue it. The reaffirmation, legal expression, and coordinated enforcement of shared multilateral norms can be one of the most powerful tools for rallying many states to the purpose of deterring excessive Chinese aggression. In order to remain a legitimate and respected leader of such a multilateral normative dialogue, however, the United States must demonstrate that it also abides by the rules. This conclusion has various policy implications:

- The United States should be wary of publicly questioning, or simply abrogating, bilateral or multilateral treaties, alliances, or agreements to which it is a party. The United States will want to advocate for its interests within these arrangements, but to scorn them would undermine U.S. influence in countering Chinese challenges to norms.

- The United States should move toward ratification of the UNCLOS as a reaffirmation of the role of international law in maritime disputes.
- The United States must keep in mind that unilateral or narrowly multilateral uses of military force outside strong UN endorsement—in such cases as Kosovo, Iraq, and Libya—may serve certain short-term interests, but they also degrade the U.S. standing to condemn similar uses of force by others.

U.S. Strategy Toward China and a Shared Order: Hedging Against Revisionism

The second broad component of a revised strategy toward China and the international order would be to recognize that China's growing power and ambitions could, in one of several worst-case scenarios, come to be expressed in more-belligerent forms. In particular, China's pursuit of territorial claims with regard to Taiwan and the South and East China Seas could lead to conflict. Regional states are not naive about the possible forms of Chinese muscle-flexing and continue to look to the United States to play an essential role in regional deterrence. The second component of U.S. strategy, therefore, is an effort to hedge against more-negative outcomes, which can have several components. The United States should undertake a renewed effort at regional diplomacy, both bilateral and multilateral, to set the geopolitical context for responding to Chinese assertiveness. It should acquire powerful military capabilities and warfighting concepts to enhance deterrence while avoiding unnecessarily provocative actions that could exacerbate fears in Beijing. In selected cases, notably Chinese gray zone assertiveness in the South China Sea, it should reaffirm its commitment to key norms and consider developing capabilities that counter Chinese actions in a less-escalatory, more-symmetrical manner, such as through the involvement of law enforcement vessels instead of naval ships.

Many observers have suggested or assumed that U.S. hedging actions should be primarily military in character—investing in general capabilities for a possible clash with China, bolstering the U.S. regional posture, and encouraging allied defense expenditures. Such military actions can contribute to deterrence, but our analysis leads us to conclude that the United States should pursue hedging not primarily through military posture, but through diplomacy and geopolitical maneuvering. The goal should be to *shape the context* so that it is resistant to Chinese coercion and aggression and resilient against Chinese efforts to split alliances, conduct cyber intrusions or attacks, employ information warfare, or undertake maritime coercion. A strong regional environment, based on well-accepted norms and strong bilateral and multilateral relationships, will likely have a greater long-term influence on Chinese calculations than a few more U.S. carriers or higher U.S. defense spending.

More specifically, then, this deterrent and hedging component of U.S. strategy can have a number of specific elements:

The United States should nurture U.S. regional influence through expanded diplomatic engagements with regional states and a growing set of engagements with nonstate actors. This recommendation is straightforward and the focus of much current U.S. policy, but our research reemphasizes the importance of preserving U.S. power, relationships, and influence as a persistent counterweight to Chinese ambitions and the essential foundation of a strategy for shaping the geopolitical context. As China builds its challenge to the current order, it will feel constrained—or not—in part by the degree of U.S. influence that remains. This recommendation points to a number of specific actions:

- Build cooperation with China to promote shared interests and counter shared threats, such as maritime piracy.
- Support regional trade agreements that link countries together, such as the Trans-Pacific Partnership.
- Sustain bilateral U.S. alliances and expand partnerships with countries.
- Continue and, in selected cases, expand bilateral and multilateral assistance programs and capacity-building networks, as well as military-to-military contacts and exercises, where possible, with allies and partners for both China and the United States.

The United States should continue to support multilateral security arrangements in Asia, including but not limited to U.S. alliances. Broadly speaking, regional states share the essential U.S. goal of avoiding hegemonic, coercive Chinese control over East Asia. Stronger multilateral organizations and processes, from U.S. alliances to ASEAN and its various offshoots to a rejuvenated Trans-Pacific Partnership, would strengthen the region's resilience against Chinese coercion in a way that was not U.S.-centric and that increasingly placed the voices of leading regional states, from Japan to South Korea to Vietnam, in the forefront of the discussion.

In the process, if and when Chinese belligerence increases, such institutions and their associated norms would allow the United States to highlight the differences between China and other major players in the order. China is increasingly reacting to not one but two overlapping regional and global orders: the U.S.-led order of alliances and the broader liberal international order. To the extent that China's dissatisfaction appears to target U.S. interests and preferences, it will gain a certain legitimacy, at least in the eyes of others not completely satisfied with the current distribution of power. However, when China's revisionism appears to target shared institutions, norms, and interests, it will generate balancing reactions from many states who see their interests tied up in the order.

A third component of a U.S. hedging strategy is to *sustain a sufficient U.S. regional posture to render large-scale aggression or territorial conquest infeasible.* The detailed requirements of such a role have been spelled out in many other sources.[7] For the time being, China continues to perceive a significant U.S. advantage in a major conflict. Many analyses have suggested that the balance is shifting over time, especially with the deployment of Chinese area-denial capabilities and particularly with regard to a potential Taiwan scenario so close to the Chinese mainland. The United States will need continued investments to sustain a credible regional deterrent, but the baseline requirement is

---

[7]   Terrence Kelly, David C. Gompert, and Duncan Long, *Smarter Power, Stronger Partners, Volume I: Exploiting U.S. Advantages to Prevent Aggression*, Santa Monica, Calif.: RAND Corporation, RR-1359-A, 2016.

to make aggression unacceptably costly, not to persist with a form of dominance that is no longer in the cards.

Yet, a fourth principle of hedging, of nearly equal importance to the persistence of U.S. regional military power, is that the United States should undertake its deterrent mission in a way that does not unnecessarily deepen Chinese fears of U.S. power and contribute to its dissatisfaction. This points to one of the most challenging but urgent priorities for U.S. regional military deterrent posture: *to develop less provocative, "defensive defense" approaches to deterring Chinese military aggression.* This general rule would downplay provocative doctrines, such as the proposed "air-sea battle" approach of striking deep into the Chinese mainland, and instead favor "Blue anti-access/area-denial" approaches of building highly effective defenses against long-distance Chinese power projection.[8]

Another important component of a hedging strategy is that *the United States should develop more-elaborated nonmilitary strategies for responding to Chinese maritime coercion.* The full scope of this challenge is beyond the scope of this report, but finding potent yet nonescalatory means with which to counteract Chinese gradual forms of assertive territorial claims will provide an important tool for dealing with a potentially worsening rivalry. Finding ways to involve the U.S. Coast Guard and other nonmilitary services or to help build the coast guard capacities of partner nations can help signal U.S. resolve in a manner that reduces the risk of escalation.[9] The United States can be clearer about the specific thresholds that it considers unacceptable, such as the direct use of force against the maritime assets of other claimants. It can also develop a strategy of multiple stages of responses: building a general global norm against certain categories of such gray zone aggression and developing a menu of response options to deploy against specific Chinese violations.

---

8   Kelly, Gompert, and Long, 2016.

9   On the challenge, see Michael Green, Kathleen Hicks, John Schaus, Jake Douglas, and Zack Cooper, *Countering Coercion in Maritime Asia: The Theory and Practice of Gray Zone Deterrence*, Washington, D.C.: Center for Strategic and International Studies, May 2017.

References

Almond, Roncevert Ganon, "China and the Iran Nuclear Deal," *The Diplomat*, March 8, 2016.

American Bar Association, "Re: Section 301 Investigation: China's Acts, Policies, and Practices Related to Technology Transfer, Intellectual Property, and Innovation," submission to the Office of the U.S. Trade Representative, September 27, 2017. As of February 28, 2018:
https://www.americanbar.org/content/dam/aba/administrative/intellectual_property_law/advocacy/advocacy-20171927-comments.authcheckdam.pdf

Asia Maritime Transparency Initiative, "China Island Tracker," webpage, Center for Strategic and International Studies, undated. As of October 1, 2017:
https://amti.csis.org/island-tracker/china/

Associated Press, "Human Rights in China Under Xi Worst Since Tiananmen: Amnesty," *South China Morning Post*, November 17, 2017. As of February 26, 2018:
http://www.scmp.com/news/china/policies-politics/article/2120318/human-rights-china-under-xi-jinping-worst-tiananmen

Astartia, Claudia, "China's Role in Southeast Asian Regional Organizations," *China Perspectives*, Vol. 3, 2008.

"At the 27th Collective Study Session of the CCP Political Bureau; Xi Jinping Stresses the Need to Push Forward the System of Global Governance," *Xinhua*, October 13, 2015.

Bader, Jeffrey A., "How Xi Jinping Sees the World . . . and Why," *Order from Chaos: Foreign Policy in a Troubled World*, Asia Working Group, Brookings Institution, February 2016. As of October 1, 2017:
https://www.brookings.edu/wp-content/uploads/2016/07/xi_jinping_worldview_bader-1.pdf

Berger, Bernt, and Philip Schell, "Toeing the Line, Drawing the Line: China and Iran's Nuclear Ambitions," *China Report*, Vol. 49, No. 1, 2013.

Bergsten, C. Fred, "A Partnership of Equals: How Washington Should Respond to China's Economic Challenge," *Foreign Affairs*, June 1, 2008. As of October 1, 2017:
https://www.foreignaffairs.com/print/1110531

Blackwill, Robert, and Ashley Tellis, "A New U.S. Grand Strategy Towards China," *The National Interest*, April 13, 2015. As of October 1, 2017:
http://nationalinterest.org/feature/wake-america-china-must-be-contained-12616

Bower, Ernest, "China Reveals Its Hand on ASEAN in Phnomn Penh," Washington, D.C.: Center for Strategic and International Studies, July 20, 2012. As of October 1, 2017:
http://csis.org/publication/china-reveals-its-hand-asean-phnom-penh

Brady, Anne-Marie, "China's Foreign Propaganda Machine," Wilson Center, Kissinger Institute on China and the United States, October 26, 2015. As of February 27, 2018:
https://www.wilsoncenter.org/article/chinas-foreign-propaganda-machine

———, "Magic Weapons: China's Political Influence Strategies Under Xi Jinping," Wilson Center, Kissinger Institute on China and the United States, September 18, 2017. As of February 27, 2018:
https://www.wilsoncenter.org/article/
magic-weapons-chinas-political-influence-activities-under-xi-jinping

Brennan, Elliott, "South China Sea: Beijing Outmaneuvers ASEAN, Again," Lowy Institute, August 6, 2015. As of February 28, 2018:
https://www.realcleardefense.com/articles/2015/08/05/south_china_sea_beijing_outmaneuvers_asean_again_108334.html

Cadell, Catherine, "China's Xi Urges Cooperation Among Nations in Governance of Global Internet," Reuters, November 16, 2016. As of February 7, 2017:
http://www.reuters.com/article/us-china-internet-idUSKBN13B1FF

Callahan, William, "Chinese Visions of World Order: Post-Hegemonic or a New Hegemony?" *International Studies Review*, No. 10, 2008.

———, "Sino-Speak: Chinese Exceptionalism and the Politics of History," *The Journal of Asian Studies*, Vol. 71, No. 1, 2012.

Campbell, Charlie, "Why an Unlikely Hero Like China Could End Up Leading the World in the Fight Against Climate Change," *Time*, June 1, 2017.

Canrong, Jin, "Tremendous Changes in International Politics and their Influence on China," *Contemporary International Relations* [现代国际关系], December 20, 2009.

Chan, Gerald, "China and the WTO: The Theory and Practice of Compliance," Chatham House, Asia Programme, Working Paper No. 5, June 2003.

Chance, Alek, "How America and China Have Different Visions of International Order," *The Diplomat*, July 3, 2015. As of October 1, 2017: http://thediplomat.com/2015/07/ how-america-and-china-have-different-visions-of-international-order/

Chang, Chris King-Chi, and Kalid Nadvi, "Changing Labour Regulations and Labour Standards in China: Retrospect and Challenges," *International Labour Review*, Vol. 153, No. 4, 2014.

Chang, Liu, "Commentary: U.S. Fiscal Failure Warrants a De-Americanized World," *Xinhua*, October 13, 2013.

Chase, Michael, "China's Search for a New Type of Great Power Relationship," *China Brief*, September 7, 2012. As of October 1, 2017: http://www.jamestown.org/single/?no_cache=1&tx_ttnews%5Btt_ news%5D=39820#.VskU_lK9bww

Chen, Zheng, "China and the Responsibility to Protect," *Journal of Contemporary China*, Vol. 25, 2016, pp.686–700.

Chin, Gregory, and Ramesh Thakur, "Will China Changes the Rules of Global Order?" *Washington Quarterly*, Vol. 33, No. 4, October 2010.

Chin, John J., "China's Militarized Interstate Dispute Behavior, 1949–2001: A Second Cut at the Data," unpublished manuscript, March 11, 2013. As of October 1, 2017: https://www.princeton.edu/politics/about/file-repository/public/Chin-China-MIDs-Paper_2013.03.11.pdf

"China, Africa Have Always Been Community of Common Destiny: Xi," *Xinhua*, December 4, 2015.

ChinaPower, "Is China Contributing to the United Nations' Mission?" Center for Strategic and International Studies, 2016. As of October 1, 2017: http://chinapower.csis.org/china-un-mission/

"China, Russia Sign Joint Statement on Strengthening Global Strategic Stability," *Xinhua*, June 27, 2016.

"China Supports, Contributes to Postwar International Order," *Xinhua*, July 30, 2015.

"China, U.S. Affirm Commitment to Continue Cooperation, Manage Differences as Talks Open," *Xinhua*, June 24, 2015.

Chinese Foreign Ministry, "Xi Jinping: Let the Community of Common Destiny Take Deep Root in Neighboring Countries," October 25, 2013. As of October 1, 2017: http://www.fmprc.gov.cn/mfa_eng/wjb_663304/wjbz_663308/activities_663312/ t1093870.shtml

———, "Xi's Speech at 'Five Principles of Peaceful Coexistence' Anniversary," July 7, 2014a. As of February 28, 2018:
http://www.china.org.cn/world/2014-07/07/content_32876905.htm

———, "The Central Conference on Work Related to Foreign Affairs Was Held in Beijing," webpage, Ministry of Foreign Relations, November 2014b. As of October 1, 2017:
http://www.fmprc.gov.cn/mfa_eng/zxxx_662805/t1215680.shtml

Chorev, Nitsan, and Sarah Babb, "The Crisis of Neoliberalism and the Future of International Institutions: A Comparison of the IMF and the WTO," *Theory and Society*, Vol. 38, No. 5, 2009.

Christensen, Thomas J., "Fostering Stability or Creating a Monster? The Rise of China and U.S. Policy Toward East Asia," *International Security*, Vol. 31, No. 1, 2006.

———, *The China Challenge: Shaping the Choices of a Rising Power*, New York: W. W. Norton, 2016.

Cole, J. Michael, "Taiwan Confirms China's 'Black Hand' Behind Anti-Democracy Protests," *Taiwan Democracy Bulletin*, Vol. 1, No. 10, July 18, 2017a.

———, "Will China's Information War Destabilize Taiwan?" *National Interest*, July 30, 2017b.

Combes, Katherine, "Between Revisionism and Status Quo: China in International Regimes," *Polis*, Vol. 6, Winter 2011–2012.

Commission on the Theft of American Intellectual Property, *Update to the IP Commission Report*, Washington, D.C.: National Bureau of Asian Research, 2017. As of February 28, 2018:
http://www.ipcommission.org/report/IP_Commission_Report_Update_2017.pdf

"Commentary: Who Is Challenging International Order?" *Xinhua*, February 1, 2016.

Correlates of War Project, homepage, undated-a. As of March 13, 2018:
http://www.correlatesofwar.org/

Correlates of War Project, "Militarized Interstate Disputes (v4.1)," webpage, undated-b. As of March 13, 2018:
http://www.correlatesofwar.org/data-sets/MIDs

Cox, Michael, "Power Shifts, Economic Change, and the Decline of the West?" webpage, United Kingdom Foreign and Commonwealth Office, November 28, 2012. As of October 1, 2017:
https://www.gov.uk/government/publications/power-shifts-economic-change-and-the-decline-of-the-west/power-shifts-economic-change-and-the-decline-of-the-west

Crothall, Geoffrey, "Refusing to Honor Labor Rights Backfires on China," *New York Times*, May 12, 2016.

Cui, Li, "China's Growing Trade Dependence," *Finance and Development*, IMF, September 2007. As of October 1, 2017:
http://www.imf.org/external/pubs/ft/fandd/2007/09/cui.htm

Danaher, Kevin, ed., *50 Years Is Enough: The Case Against the World Bank*, New York: South End Press, 1999.

De Grauwe, Paul, and Zhaoyong Zhang, "The Rise of China and Regional Integration in East Asia," *Scottish Journal of Political Economy*, Vol. 63, No. 1, 2016.

Deng, Yong, "Hegemon on the Offensive: Chinese Perspectives on U. S. Global Strategy," *Political Science Quarterly*, Vol. 116, No. 3, 2001. As of October 1, 2017:
www.jstor.org/stable/798020

———, "China: The Post-Responsible Power," *Washington Quarterly*, Vol. 37, No. 4, Winter 2015.

Denyer, Simon, "China's Rise and Asian Tensions Send U.S. Relations into Downward Spiral," *Washington Post*, July 7, 2014. As of February 27, 2018:
https://www.washingtonpost.com/world/asia_pacific/chinas-rise-and-asian-tensions-send-us-relations-into-downward-spiral/2014/07/07/f371cfaa-d5cd-4dd2-925c-246c099f04ed_story.html

Dingding, Chen, "China's Participation in the International Human Rights Regime: A State Identity Perspective," *Chinese Journal of International Politics*, Vol. 2, No. 3, July 2009.

Duchâtel, Mathieu, and Bates Gill, "Overseas Citizen Protection: A Growing Challenge for China," *SIPRI Newsletter*, February 2012. As of January 14, 2016:
www.sipri.org/media/newsletter/essay/february12

Easterly, William, *The Elusive Quest for Growth*, Cambridge, Mass.: MIT Press, 2001.

———, *White Man's Burden: Why the West's Efforts to Aid the Rest Have Done So Much Ill and So Little Good*, New York: Penguin Books, 2007.

Economy, Elizabeth C., "Beijing Is No Champion of Globalization," *Foreign Affairs*, January 22, 2017.

———, "Why China Is No Climate Leader," *Politico*, June 12, 2017.

Estlund, Cynthia, "A New Deal for China's Workers?" Cambridge, Mass.: Harvard University Press, 2017.

Etzioni, Amitai, and G. John Ikenberry, "Is China More Westphalian Than the West?" *Foreign Affairs*, October 17, 2011. As of October 1, 2017:
https://www.foreignaffairs.com/print/1069711

Etzioni, Amitai, "How Aggressive Is China?" *Korean Journal of International Studies*, Vol. 14, No. 2, August 2016.

Fang, Xie, "Rethinking Tianxia," Workshop Report, *China Heritage Quarterly*, No. 26, June 2011. As of October 1, 2017: http://www.chinaheritagequarterly.org/tien-hsia.php?searchterm=026_tianxia. inc&issue=026

Feng, Bree, "Obama's 'Free Rider' Comment Draws Chinese Criticism," *New York Times*, August 13, 2014. As of February 27, 2018: https://sinosphere.blogs.nytimes.com/2014/08/13/ obamas-free-rider-comment-draws-chinese-criticism/

Ferchen, Matt, "The Contradictions of China's Developing Country Identity," Carnegie-Tsinghua Center for Global Policy, June 13, 2014. As of October 1, 2017: http://carnegietsinghua.org/2014/06/13/ contradictions-of-china-s-developing-country-identity-pub-55938

Ferdinand, Peter, "Rising Powers at the UN: An Analysis of the Voting Behavior of BRICS in the General Assembly," *Third World Quarterly*, Vol. 35, No. 3, 2014.

Fine, Ben, Costas Lapavitsas, and Jonathan Pincus, *Development Policy in the 21st Century: Beyond the Post-Washington Consensus*, London: Routledge, 2001.

Fingar, Thomas, "China's Vision of World Order," in *Strategic Asia 2012-2013: China's Military Challenge*, Ashley J. Tellis and Travis Tanner, eds., Seattle, Wash.: National Bureau of Asian Research, 2012.

Francis, David, "IMF Officially Gives China Seat at the Adult Table of World Economics," *Foreign Policy*, October 3, 2016.

Fravel, M. Taylor, "Regime Insecurity and International Cooperation: Explaining China's Compromises in Territorial Disputes," *International Security*, Vol. 30, No. 2, 2005.

———, *Strong Borders, Secure Nation: Cooperation and Conflicts in China's Territorial Disputes*, Princeton, N.J.: Princeton University Press, 2008.

Frieman, Wendy, *China, Arms Control and Nonproliferation*, London: Routledge, 2004.

Frost, Ellen, "China's Activities in Southeast Asia and the Implications for U.S. Interests—Panel V: China and Regional Forums," Washington, D.C., testimony before the U.S.-China Economic and Security Review Commission, February 4, 2010. As of February 26, 2018: https://www.uscc.gov/Hearings/ hearing-china%E2%80%99s-activities-southeast-asia-and-implications-us-interests

"Full Text of Hu Jintao's Report at 18th Party Congress," *Xinhua*, November 2012.

"Full Text of Xi Jinping's Report to the 19th Party Congress," *Xinhua*, November 3, 2017.

Fung, Courtney J., "China and the Responsibility to Protect: From Opposition to Advocacy," United States Institute of Peace, *PeaceBrief*, No. 205, June 2016.

Global Times, "China Takes on Global Responsibility at G-20," August 3, 2015. As of February 28, 2018:
http://www.globaltimes.cn/content/935250.shtml

Godement, François, "China's Promotion of a Low-Cost International Order," commentary, European Council on Foreign Relations, May 6, 2015. As of February 28, 2018:
http://www.ecfr.eu/article/
commentary_chinas_promotion_of_a_low_cost_international_order3017

Grant, Charles, *Russia, China and Global Governance*, Centre for European Reform, 2012. As of October 1, 2017:
https://www.cer.org.uk/sites/default/files/publications/attachments/pdf/2012/rp_072_km-6279.pdf

Green, Michael, Kathleen Hicks, John Schaus, Jake Douglas, and Zack Cooper, *Countering Coercion in Maritime Asia: The Theory and Practice of Gray Zone Deterrence*, Washington, D.C.: Center for Strategic and International Studies, May 2017.

Griffiths, Ryan D., "The Future of Self-Determination and Territorial Integrity in the Asian Century," *Pacific Review*, Vol. 27, No. 3, 2014.

———, "States, Nations, and Territorial Stability: Why Chinese Hegemony Would Be Better for International Order," *Security Studies*, Vol. 25, No. 3, 2016.

Gunness, Kristen, *PLA Expeditionary Capabilities and Implications for United States Asia Policy*, Santa Monica, Calif.: RAND Corporation, CT-452, 2016. As of February 24, 2018:
https://www.rand.org/pubs/testimonies/CT452.html

Harold, Scott W., Martin C. Libicki, and Astrid Stuth Cevallos, *Getting to Yes with China in Cyberspace*, Santa Monica, Calif.: RAND Corporation, RR-1335-RC, 2016. As of February 24, 2018:
https://www.rand.org/pubs/research_reports/RR1335.html

Heath, Timothy R., "China and the U.S. Alliance System," *The Diplomat*, July 11, 2014a. As of October 1, 2017:
http://thediplomat.com/2014/06/china-and-the-u-s-alliance-system/

———, "China's Big Diplomacy Shift," *The Diplomat*, December 22, 2014b. As of October 1, 2017:
http://thediplomat.com/2014/12/chinas-big-diplomacy-shift/

———, "China Intensifies Effort to Establish Leading Role in Asia, Dislodge U.S.," *China Brief*, Vol. 17, No. 2, February 6, 2017.

Heath, Timothy R., and Andrew S. Erickson, "Is China Pursuing Counter Intervention?" *Washington Quarterly*, October 30, 2015. As of October 1, 2017: http://www.tandfonline.com/doi/full/10.1080/0163660X.2015.1099029

Heginbotham, Eric, Michael Nixon, Forrest E. Morgan, Jacob Heim, Jeff Hagen, Sheng Tao Li, Jeffrey Engstrom, Martin C. Libicki, Paul DeLuca, David A. Shlapak, David R. Frelinger, Burgess Laird, Kyle Brady, and Lyle J. Morris, *The U.S.-China Military Scorecard: Forces, Geography, and the Evolving Balance of Power, 1996–2017*, Santa Monica, Calif.: RAND Corporation, RR-392-AF, 2015. As of February 28, 2018: https://www.rand.org/pubs/research_reports/RR392.html

Heilmann, Sebastian, Moritz Rudolph, Mikko Huotari, and Johannes Buckow, "China's Shadow Foreign Policy," Mercator Institute for China Studies, No. 18, October 2014.

Hernandez, Diego, "Are 'New' Donors Challenging World Bank Conditionality?" *AidData*, Working Paper 19, January 2016.

Horsburgh, Nicola, *China and Global Nuclear Order: From Estrangement to Active Engagement*, Cambridge, UK: Cambridge University Press, 2015.

Houlewig, Henk, "Power Transition as a Cause of War," *Journal of Conflict Resolution*, Vol. 32, March 1988.

Hsueh, Roselyn, "Why Is China Suddenly Leading the Climate Change Effort? It's a Business Decision," *Washington Post*, June 2, 2017.

"Hu Jintao Calls for Harmonious Asia," *Xinhua*, June 17, 2006.

Human Rights Watch, *World Report 2017, Events of 2016: China*, New York, 2017. As of October 1, 2017: https://www.hrw.org/world-report/2017/country-chapters/china-and-tibet

Ikenberry, G. John, *After Wars: Institutions, Strategic Restraint, and the Rebuilding of Order After Major Wars*, Princeton, N.J.: Princeton University Press, 2000.

⸺, *After Victory: Institutions, Strategic Restraint, and the Rebuilding of Order After Major Wars*, Princeton, N.J.: Princeton University Press, 2001.

Ikenberry, G. John, and Darren Lim, "China's Emerging Institutional Statecraft," Brookings Institution, April 2017. As of October 1, 2017: https://www.brookings.edu/research/chinas-emerging-institutional-statecraft/

IMF—*See* International Monetary Fund.

Information Office of the State Council, "China's Peaceful Development," white paper, People's Republic of China, September 21, 2011. As of October 1, 2017: http://english1.english.gov.cn/official/2011-09/06/content_1941354.htm

International Crisis Group, "China's Foreign Policy Experiment in South Sudan," Report No. 288, July 10, 2017. As of February 28, 2018:
https://www.crisisgroup.org/africa/horn-africa/
south-sudan/288-china-s-foreign-policy-experiment-south-sudan

"The International Law Ironies of US Provocations in the South China Sea," *Xinhua*, January 31, 2016.

International Monetary Fund, "IMF Survey: Chinese Renminbi to Be Included in IMF's Special Drawing Right Basket," IMF Survey, December 1, 2015. As of October 1, 2017:
https://www.imf.org/en/News/Articles/2015/09/28/04/53/sonew120115a

Jacobs, Andrew, "China Urges Quick End to Airstrikes in Libya," *New York Times*, March 22, 2011. As of February 27, 2018:
http://www.nytimes.com/2011/03/23/world/asia/23beiijing.html

Jacques, Martin, *When China Rules the World*, New York: Penguin Books, 2012.

Jain, Romi, "China's Compliance with the WTO: A Critical Examination," *Indian Journal of International Affairs*, Vol. 29, No. 1–2, June–December 2016.

Jiechi, Yang, "China's Interaction with the World in the New Era," *Research in International Problems* [国际问题研究], September 13, 2011.

Jiemian, Yang, "U.S. Soft Power and the Reorganization of the International System," *Research in International Problems* [国际问题研究], March 13, 2012.

Jinping, Xi, "Full Text from President Xi Jinping's Speech," New York City, National Committee on U.S.-China Relations, September 2015a. As of October 1, 2017:
https://www.ncuscr.org/content/full-text-president-xi-jinpings-speech

———, "Working Together to Forge a New Partnership of Win-Win Cooperation and Create a Community of Shared Future for Mankind," speech at the General Debate of the 70th Session of the UN General Assembly, New York, September 28, 2015b. As of October 1, 2017:
https://gadebate.un.org/sites/default/files/gastatements/70/70_ZH_en.pdf

———, "Secure a Decisive Victory in Building a Moderately Prosperous Society in All Respects and Strive for the Great Success of Socialism with Chinese Characteristics for a New Era," speech to the 19th National Congress of the Communist Party of China, October 18, 2017.

Johnston, Alastair Iain, "China's Militarized Interstate Dispute Behavior, 1949–1992: A First Cut at the Data," *China Quarterly*, No. 153, 1998.

———, *Social States: China in International Institutions, 1980–2000*, Princeton, N.J.: Princeton University Press, 2008.

———, "How New and Assertive Is China's New Assertiveness?" *International Security*, Vol. 37, No. 4, Spring 2013.

————, "China and International Order: Which China? Which Order?" paper presented at the conference "Negotiating the Future: Visions of Global Order," German Institute of Global and Area Studies, Hamburg, Germany, December 3–4, 2015.

Kan, Shirley, *China and Proliferation of Weapons of Mass Destruction and Missiles: Policy Issues*, Washington, D.C.: Congressional Research Service, RL31555, January 5, 2015. As of February 26, 2018:
https://fas.org/sgp/crs/nuke/RL31555.pdf

Kelly, Terrence, James Dobbins, David A. Shlapak, David C. Gompert, Eric Heginbotham, Peter Chalk, and Lloyd Thrall, *The U.S. Army in Asia, 2030–2040*, Santa Monica, Calif.: RAND Corporation, RR-474-A, 2014. As of February 28, 2018:
https://www.rand.org/pubs/research_reports/RR474.html

Kelly, Terrence, David C. Gompert, and Duncan Long, *Smarter Power, Stronger Partners, Volume I: Exploiting U.S. Advantages to Prevent Aggression*, Santa Monica, Calif: RAND Corporation, RR-1359-A, 2016. As of March 1, 2018:
https://www.rand.org/pubs/research_reports/RR1359.html.

Kent, Ann, "China's International Socialization: The Role of International Organizations," *Global Governance*, Vol. 8, No. 3, July–September 2002.

Khong, Yuen Foong, "Primacy or World Order? The United States and China's Rise—A Review Essay," *International Security*, Vol. 38, No. 3, Winter 2013–2014.

Kurlantzick, Joshua, "Beijing's Safari: China's Move into Africa and Its Implications for Aid, Development, and Governance," Carnegie Endowment for International Peace, November 2006. As of October 1, 2017:
http://carnegieendowment.org/files/kurlantzick_outlook_africa2.pdf

————, *Democracy in Retreat: The Revolt of the Middle Class and Worldwide Decline in Representative Government*, New Haven, Conn.: Yale University Press, 2013.

Lanteigne, Marc, *China and International Institutions: Alternate Paths to Global Power*, London: Routledge, 2005.

Larson, Deborah Welch, and Alexei Shevchenko, "Status Seekers: Chinese and Russian Responses to U.S. Primacy," *International Security*, Vol. 34, No. 4, Spring 2010.

Leng, Chua Chin, "The Politics of Non-Interference—A New World Order," *China Daily*, January 25, 2016

Levin, Dan, "At U.N., China Tries to Influence Fight Over Internet Control," *New York Times*, December 16, 2015. As of February 28, 2018:
https://www.nytimes.com/2015/12/17/technology/china-wins-battle-with-un-over-word-in-internet-control-document.html

Liff, Adam P., "China and the U.S. Alliance System," *China Quarterly*, Vol. 233, April 2017, pp. 137–165.

Limin, Lin, "China's Foreign Strategy: New Problems, New Tasks, New Ideas," *Contemporary International Relations* [现代国际关系], November 20, 2010.

Liping, Xia, "Nuclear Nonproliferation from a Chinese Perspective," Bonn, Germany: *Friedrich Ebert Stiftung*, Shanghai Briefing Paper No. 8, 2008.

Lum, Thomas, Hannah Fischer, Julissa Gomez-Granger, and Anne Leland, *China's Foreign Aid Activities in Africa, Latin America, and Southeast Asia*, Washington, D.C.: Congressional Research Service, R40361, February 25, 2009. As of October 1, 2017:
https://fas.org/sgp/crs/row/R40361.pdf

Lynch, Colum, "China Eyes Ending Western Grip on Top UN Jobs with Greater Control Over Blue Helmets," *Foreign Policy*, October 2, 2016.

Malik, J. Mohan, "China and the Nuclear Non-Proliferation Regime," *Contemporary Southeast Asia*, Vol. 22, No. 3, 2000.

Martin, Lisa, "Against Compliance," American Political Science Association, annual meeting paper, 2011. As of October 1, 2017:
https://ssrn.com/abstract=1900163

Mastro, Oriana Skylar, "China's Military Is About to Go Global," *National Interest*, December 18, 2014. As of October 1, 2017:
http://nationalinterest.org/feature/chinas-military-about-go-global-11882

———, "A Global People's Liberation Army: Possibilities, Challenges, and Opportunities," *Asia Policy*, July 2016.

Mattis, Peter, "Contrasting China's and Russia's Influence Operations," *War on the Rocks*, January 16, 2018.

Mauldin, William, "U.S. Begins Formal Probe of China Technology Transfer," *Wall Street Journal*, August 18, 2017. As of February 26, 2018:
https://www.wsj.com/articles/u-s-formally-begins-probe-of-china-technology-transfer-1503091630

Mazarr, Michael J., "Preserving the Postwar Order," *Washington Quarterly*, Vol. 40, No. 2, Summer 2017.

Mazarr, Michael J., Miranda Priebe, Andrew Radin, and Astrid Stuth Cevallos, *Understanding the Current International Order*, Santa Monica, Calif.: RAND Corporation, RR-1598-OSD, 2016. As of February 25, 2018:
https://www.rand.org/pubs/research_reports/RR1598.html

———, *Alternative Options for U.S. Policy Toward the International Order*, Santa Monica, Calif.: RAND Corporation, RR-2011-OSD, 2017. As of February 27, 2018:
https://www.rand.org/pubs/research_reports/RR2011.html

Mazarr, Michael J., and Ashley L. Rhoades, *Testing the Value of the Postwar International Order*, Santa Monica, Calif.: RAND Corporation, RR-2226-OSD, 2018. As of February 24, 2018:
https://www.rand.org/pubs/research_reports/RR2226.html

McDowell, Daniel, "New Order: China's Challenge to the Global Financial System," *World Politics Review*, April 14, 2015.

Medeiros, Evan S., *China's International Behavior: Activism, Opportunism, and Diversification*, Santa Monica, Calif.: RAND Corporation, MG-850-AF, 2009. As of February 28, 2018:
https://www.rand.org/pubs/monographs/MG850.html

Melnicoe, Mark, "China: New Labor Laws Seek to Pressure Chinese Employers," *Bloomberg BNA*, February 6, 2017.

Mesbahi, Mohiaddin, and Mohammed Homayounvash, "China and the International Nonproliferation Regime: The Case of Iran," *Sociology of Islam*, Vol. 4, No. 1–2, 2016.

Ministry of Foreign Affairs of the People's Republic of China, "Joint Statement of the People's Republic of China and the Russian Federation on Major International Issues," webpage, May 23, 2008. As of October 1, 2017:
http://www.fmprc.gov.cn/mfa_eng/wjdt_665385/2649_665393/t465821.shtml

———, "Foreign Ministry Spokesperson Lu Kang's Regular Press Conference on July 13, 2016," webpage, July 13, 2016. As of October 1, 2017:
http://www.fmprc.gov.cn/mfa_eng/xwfw_665399/s2510_665401/t1381285.shtml

Montinola, Gabriela, "When Does Aid Conditionality Work?" *Studies for Comparative International Development*, Vol. 45, No. 3, 2010, pp. 358–382.

Mozur, Paul, and Jane Perlez, "China Bets on Sensitive U.S. Start-Ups, Worrying the Pentagon," *New York Times*, March 22, 2017a.

———, "China Tech Investment Flying Under the Radar, Pentagon Warns," *New York Times*, April 7, 2017b.

Nathan, Andrew J., "Authoritarian Resilience," Journal of Democracy, Vol. 14, No. 1, January 2003.

———, "China's Rise and International Regimes: Does China Seek to Overthrow Global Norms?" in Robert S. Ross and Jo Inge Bekkevold, eds., *China in the Era of Xi Jinping: Domestic and Foreign Policy Challenges*, Washington, D.C.: Georgetown University Press, 2016.

Nippert, Matt, and David Fisher, "Revealed: China's Network of Influence in New Zealand," *New Zealand Herald*, January 17, 2018.

Noesselt, Nele, "Is There a 'Chinese School' of IR?" German Institute of Global and Area Studies, Working Paper No. 188, March 2012. As of October 1, 2017:
https://giga.hamburg/en/system/files/publications/wp188_noesselt.pdf

Norris, William J., *Chinese Economic Statecraft: Commercial Actors, Grand Strategy, and State Control*, Ithaca, N.Y.: Cornell University Press, 2016.

Nunez, Christina, "China Poised for Leadership on Climate Change After U.S. Reversal," *National Geographic*, March 28, 2017.

Nye, Joseph, "The Limits of Chinese Soft Power," Project Syndicate, July 2015.

Office of the U.S. Trade Representative, *2002 Report to Congress on China's WTO Compliance*, December 11, 2002.

———, *2015 Report to Congress on China's WTO Compliance*, December 2015. As of October 1, 2017:
https://ustr.gov/sites/default/files/2015-Report-to-Congress-China-WTO-Compliance.pdf

———, *2017 Special 301 Report*, April 2017. As of February 26, 2018:
https://ustr.gov/sites/default/files/301/2017%20Special%20301%20Report%20FINAL.PDF

Olson, Stephen, and Clyde Prestowitz, *The Evolving Role of China in International Institutions*, U.S.-China Economic and Security Review Commission, January 2011. As of October 1, 2017:
https://www.uscc.gov/sites/default/files/Research/TheEvolvingRoleofChinainInternationalInstitutions.pdf

Party Committee Central Group of the Ministry of Foreign Affairs, "The New Realm of Diplomatic Theory of Socialism with Chinese Characteristics," *Seeking Truth* [求是], February 16, 2013.

Paul, T. V., Deborah Welch Larson, and William C. Wohlforth, *Status in World Politics*, New York: Cambridge University Press, 2014.

People's Republic of China Ministry of National Defense, "Defense Ministry's Regular Press Conference on May 26," May 26, 2016. As of October 1, 2017:
http://eng.mod.gov.cn/Press/2016-05/26/content_4665371.htm

Perlez, Jane, "China Creates a World Bank of Its Own, and the U.S. Balks," *New York Times*, December 4, 2015. As of February 26, 2018:
https://www.nytimes.com/2015/12/05/business/international/china-creates-an-asian-bank-as-the-us-stands-aloof.html

———, "Tribunal Rejects Beijing's Claims in South China Sea," *New York Times*, July 12, 2016.

Permanent Mission of the People's Republic of China to the United Nations, "China's Position on the War in Iraq," March 26, 2003. As of October 1, 2017:
http://www.china-un.org/eng/chinaandun/securitycouncil/regionalhotspots/mideast/ylk/t537117.htm

Pillsbury, Michael, *The Hundred Year Marathon: China's Secret Strategy to Replace America as the Global Superpower*, New York: Henry Holt and Co., 2015.

Poh, Angela, "The Myth of Chinese Sanctions over South China Sea Disputes," *Washington Quarterly*, Vol. 40, No. 1, Spring 2017.

Rapkin, David, and William Thompson, *Transition Scenarios: China and the United States in the Twenty-First Century*, Chicago: University of Chicago Press, 2013.

Raustiala, Karl, and Anne-Marie Slaughter, "International Law, International Relations and Compliance," in Walter Carlsnaes, Thomas Risse, and Beth A. Simmons, eds., *Handbook of International Relations*, London: Sage Publications, 2002.

Redden, Elizabeth, "China's 'Long Arm,'" *Inside Higher Education*, January 3, 2018.

"Remarks at the Fourth Summit of the Conference on Interaction and Confidence Building Measures (CICA)," *Xinhua*, May 21, 2014.

Renshon, Jonathan, *Fighting for Status: Hierarchy and Conflict in World Politics*, Princeton, N.J.: Princeton University Press, 2017.

Rolland, Nadège, "China's 'Belt and Road Initiative': Underwhelming or Game-Changer?" *Washington Quarterly*, Vol. 40, No. 1, Spring 2017.

Ruggie, John Gerard, "Third Try at World Order? America and Multilateralism after the Cold War," *Political Science Quarterly*, Vol. 109, No. 4, 1994. As of October 1, 2017:
www.jstor.org/stable/2151838

Sanger, David E., and Jane Perlez, "Trump Hands the Chinese a Gift: The Chance for Global Leadership," *New York Times*, June 1, 2017. As of February 26, 2018:
https://www.nytimes.com/2017/06/01/us/politics/climate-accord-trump-china-global-leadership.html

Sceats, Sonya, and Shaun Breslin, "China and the International Human Rights System," Chatham House Report, October 2012.

Schmidt, Vivian, *The Eurozone's Crisis of Democratic Legitimacy*, Luxembourg: European Commission, European Economy Discussion Paper No. 15, 2015. As of October 1, 2017:
https://ec.europa.eu/info/sites/info/files/dp015_en.pdf

Schweller, Randall L., and Xiaoyu Pu, "After Unipolarity: China's Visions of International Order in an Era of U.S. Decline," *International Security*, Vol. 36, No. 1, Summer 2011.

Scobell, Andrew, and Scott W. Harold, "An 'Assertive' China? Insights from Interviews," *Asian Security*, Vol. 9, No. 2, 2013.

Scott, James, and Rorden Wilkinson, "China as a System Preserving Power in the WTO," in Dries Lesage and Thijs Van De Graaf, eds., *Rising Powers and Multilateral Institutions*, New York: Palgrave Macmillan, 2015.

Security Council Report, *The Security Council Veto*, New York: United Nations Security Council, December 2016. As of October 1, 2017:
http://www.securitycouncilreport.org/un-security-council-working-methods/atf/cf/%7B65BFCF9B-6D27-4E9C-8CD3-CF6E4FF96FF9%7D/working%20methods_the%20veto.pdf

Shambaugh, David, "The Illusion of Chinese Power," Brookings Institution, June 25, 2014. As of October 1, 2017:
http://www.brookings.edu/research/opinions/2014/06/23-chinese-power-shambaugh

———, "China's Campaign to Enhance Soft Power," *Foreign Affairs*, June 6, 2015.

Sheng, Zhong, "Significance of 19th CPC Congress, Promoting Community of Common Destiny," Beijing Renmin Ribao Online, November 24, 2017, p. 3.

Shilong, Yang, "The Tsinghua University Report on Global Security Forum Stresses Need to Build a Sustained, Stable International System," *Outlook* [了望], December 5, 2011, No. 49.

Small, Andrew, "How China Helped Pakistan Build the Bomb," *The Telegraph*, November 15, 2015.

Snyder, Quddus V., "Integrating Rising Powers: Liberal Systemic Theory and the Mechanism of Cooperation," *Review of International Studies*, Vol. 39, 2013.

Stewart, Ian J., "China and Non-Proliferation: Progress at Last?" *The Diplomat*, March 25, 2015.

Stewart, Phil, "U.S., China Agree to Rules for Air-to-Air Military Encounters," Reuters, September 25, 2015. As of February 27, 2018:
http://www.reuters.com/article/us-usa-china-pentagon-idUSKCN0RP1X520150925

Stewart, Terrence P., *China's Compliance with World Trade Organization Obligations: A Review of China's 1st Two Years of Membership*, Washington, D.C., report prepared for the U.S.-China Security and Economic Review Commission, March 19, 2004. As of October 1, 2017:
https://www.uscc.gov/sites/default/files/Research/china%20compliance%20with%20wto%20obligations%20first%20two%20years.pdf

Strange, Austin, Bradley Parks, Michael Tierney, Andreas Fuchs, and Axel Dreher, "Working Paper: Tracking Under-Reported Financial Flows: China's Development Finance and the Aid-Conflict Nexus Revisited," Courant Research Centre: Poverty, Equity, and Growth Discussion Papers, No. 175, 2015. As of October 1, 2017:
http://hdl.handle.net/10419/110385

Swaine, Michael D., "Perceptions of an Assertive China," *China Leadership Monitor*, No. 32, May 2010. As of October 1, 2017:
http://carnegieendowment.org/files/CLM32MS1.pdf

———, "Beyond American Predominance in the Western Pacific: The Need for a Stable U.S.-China Balance of Power," Carnegie Endowment for International Peace. April 20, 2015. As of October 1, 2017: http://carnegieendowment.org/2015/04/20/beyond-american-predominance-in-western-pacific-need-for-stable-u.s.-china-balance-of-power-pub-59837

———, "Chinese Views on Global Governance Since 2008–2009: Not Much New," *China Leadership Monitor*, February 8, 2016. As of October 1, 2017: http://carnegieendowment.org/files/CLM49MS.pdf

Tiezzi, Shannon, "Yes, the U.S. Does Want to Contain China (Sort Of)," *The Diplomat,* August 8, 2015.

Tharoor, Ishaan, "China's 'Long Arm of Influence' Stretches Ever Further," *Washington Post*, December 14, 2017.

U.S. Congressional-Executive Commission on China, "The Long Arm of China: Exporting Authoritarianism with Chinese Characteristics," December 13, 2017.

U.S. Energy Information Administration, "China," webpage, May 14, 2015. As of February 28, 2018: https://www.eia.gov/beta/international/analysis.cfm?iso=CHN

Varrall, Merriden, "Chinese World Views and China's Foreign Policy," Lowy Institute, November 26, 2015. As of October 1, 2017: https://www.lowyinstitute.org/publications/chinese-worldviews-and-china-s-foreign-policy

Vice, Margaret, "In Global Popularity Contest, U.S. and China—Not Russia—Vie for First Place," Pew Research Center, August 23, 2017. As of February 23, 2018: http://www.pewresearch.org/fact-tank/2017/08/23/in-global-popularity-contest-u-s-and-china-not-russia-vie-for-first/

Wang, Yiwei, "Public Diplomacy and the Rise of Chinese Soft Power," *Annals of the American Academy of Political and Social Science*, Vol. 616, March 2008.

Wang, Yue, "China First: Foreign Tech Firms Must Be Wary Under Xi Jinping's Rule," *Forbes*, October 23, 2017.

"Washington, Beijing Agree to Block G4 Plan," *Xinhua*, August 4, 2005.

Webster, Timothy, "Paper Compliance: How China Implements WTO Decisions," *Michigan Journal of International Law*, Vol. 35, No. 3, 2014.

Weidong, Ren, "The Crimea Crisis Speeds up Disintegration of US Hegemony," *Global Times* [环球时报], April 2, 2014.

Westbrook, Tom, "Australia, Citing Concerns about China, Cracks Down on Foreign Political Influence," Reuters, December 4, 2017.

Wolf, David, "Why Buy the Hardware When China Is Getting the IP for Free," *Foreign Policy*, April 24, 2015.

Wong, Edward, "Could China Take the Lead on Climate Change? That Could Be Difficult," *New York Times*, June 2, 2017.

Wong, Edward, and David Jolly, "China Considers Larger Role in Afghan Peace Process," *New York Times*, January 24, 2016. As of February 26, 2018: https://www.nytimes.com/2016/01/25/world/asia/china-considers-larger-role-in-afghanistan-peace-process.html

World Economic Forum, "President Xi's Speech to Davos in Full," Davos, Switzerland, keynote speech at opening session of annual meeting, January 17, 2017.

Xiang, Lanxin, "Xi's Dream and China's Future," *Survival*, Vol. 58, No. 3, June–July 2016.

"Xi Eyes More Enabling Int'l Environment for China's Peaceful Development," *Xinhua*, November 30, 2014.

"Xi Jinping Delivers Important Speech at Peripheral Diplomatic Work Forum," *Xinhua*, October 25, 2013.

"Xi Jinping Speaks at the 19th Collective Study Session of the CCP Political Bureau, Stresses Need to Accelerate Free Trade Zone Strategy," *Xinhua*, December 6, 2014.

Xinchun, Niu, "U.S.-China Relations: Collision and Competition of Ideologies," *Research in International Problems* [国际问题研究], March 13, 2012.

———, "China's Diplomacy Requires a Strategic Transformation," *Contemporary International Relations* [现代国际关系], January 2013.

Xing, Qu, "The Top Level Design and Bottom Line Thinking of Chinese Diplomacy," *International Herald Leader*, September 16, 2013.

"Xi Vows No Compromise on Core Interests," *Xinhua*, March 11, 2014.

Xuetong, Yan, "China Can Thrive in the Trump Era," *New York Times*, January 25, 2017.

Yi, Wang, "Steadfastly Maintain the Righteousness Profit Concept," *People's Daily* [人民日报], September 10, 2013. As of October 1, 2017: http://opinion.people.com.cn/n/2013/0910/c1003-22862978.html

Ying, Fu, "China and the Future of the International Order," London, speech at Chatham House, July 6, 2016a.

———, "China No Threat to International Order," China-U.S. Focus, February 15, 2016b. As of October 1, 2017: http://www.chinausfocus.com/foreign-policy/putting-the-orders-shift-in-perspective/

Ying, Li, "China's Diplomacy Matches with the Country's Status as the World's Number Two: Interview with Yan Xuetong," *International Herald Leader* [国际先驱导报], December 6, 2010. As of February 28, 2018: http://news.xinhuanet.com/herald/2010-12/06/c_13636783.htm

Yingli, Yu, "Redefining the China Model: Concepts Impacts," *Contemporary International Relations* [现代国际关系], June 20, 2010.

Yingying, Huang, "Meng Xiangqing: China Has Had Great Breakthroughs on Regional Crisis Management" [孟祥青:中国周边危机管控已有大突破], *International Herald Leader* [国际先驱导报], November 6, 2012.

Zacher, Mark W., "The Territorial Integrity Norm: International Boundaries and the Use of Force," *International Organization*, Vol. 55, No. 2, 2001.

Zaibang, Wang, "Historical Change Shows That Systematic Adjustment Is Urgent; Review of and Thoughts on the 2008 International System," *Contemporary International Relations* [现代国际关系], January 20, 2009.

Zeng, Ka, and Wei Liang, *China and Global Trade Governance: China's First Decade in the World Trade Organization*, London: Routledge, 2013.

Zhang, Feng, "The Tianxia System: World Order in a Chinese Utopia," *China Heritage Quarterly*, No. 21, March 2010.

———, "Chinese Thinking on the South China Sea and the Future of Regional Security," *Political Science Quarterly*, Vol. 132, No. 3, 2017.

Zhang, Xiaoling, "How Ready Is China for a China-Style World Order? China's State Media Discourse Under Construction," *African Journalism Studies*, Vol. 34, No. 3, 2013.

Zhang, Xiaowen, and Xiaoling Li, "The Politics of Compliance with Adverse WTO Dispute Settlement Rulings in China," *Journal of Contemporary China*, Vol. 23, No. 85, 2014.

Zheng, Sarah, "China Completes Registration of 8,000 Strong UN Peace Keeping Force, Defense Ministry Says," *South China Morning Post,* September 29, 2017.

Zhongying, Pang, "The Postwar International Order Has Changed Beyond Recognition," *Global Times* [环球时报], October 16, 2014.

Zoellick, Robert B., "Whither China: From Membership to Responsibility?" remarks to National Committee on U.S.-China Relations, New York City, September 21, 2005. As of October 1, 2017: http://2001-2009.state.gov/s/d/former/zoellick/rem/53682.htm

Zongyou, Wei, "China's Maritime Trap," *Washington Quarterly*, Vol. 40, No. 1, Spring 2017.

Zongze, Ruan, "China Should Take Part in the Rules Game," *People's Daily* [人民日报], October 15, 2012.